BERTRAND RUSSELL'S PHILOSOPHY
OF LANGUAGE

BERTRAND RUSSELL'S PHILOSOPHY OF LANGUAGE

by

ROBERT J. CLACK

MARTINUS NIJHOFF – THE HAGUE – 1969

PRINTED IN THE NETHERLANDS

TABLE OF CONTENTS

RUSSELL AND THE LINGUISTIC PHILOSOPHY

It is generally acknowledged that Bertrand Russell played a vital role in the so-called "revolution" that has taken place in twentieth century Anglo-American philosophy, the revolution that has led many philosophers virtually to equate philosophy with some variety – or varieties – of linguistic analysis. His contributions to this revolution were twofold: (1) together with G. E. Moore he led the successful revolt against the neo-Hegelianism of Idealists such as Bradley and McTaggert; (2) again with Moore he provided much of the impetus for a somewhat revolutionary way of doing philosophy. (1) and (2) are, of course, closely related, since the new way of philosophizing could be said to *constitute*, in large part, the revolt against Idealism. Be this as it may, however, the important fact for present consideration is that Russell was a major influence in turning Anglo-American philosophy in the direction it has subsequently taken – toward what may be termed, quite generally, the "linguistic philosophy."

Unfortunately, though his importance as a precursor of the linguistic philosophy is well-known, the precise sense in which Russell himself can be considered a "philosopher of language" has not, to the present time, been sufficiently clarified. Useful beginnings have been made toward an investigation of this question, but they have been, withal, only beginnings, and nothing like an adequate picture of Russell's overall philosophy of language is presently available. Still wanting is a systematic examination of the various aspects of his analytic method which, collectively, give to his philosophy of language its distinctive character.

It is such an examination that I shall attempt to provide in the present study. Specifically, I shall try to show how Russell's analytic method is rooted in a specific conception of the philosophical *purpose* of linguistic analysis and how, consequently, many of the criticisms which have recently been levelled against the type of analysis he employed are without the force they are sometimes thought to have, for they seem to be premised on an assumption that the motive behind his use of linguistic analysis was quite other than it in fact was. It is, I think, important to show this; otherwise Russell's very real contribution to contemporary philosophy in general and to the linguistic philosophy in particular may be lost sight of, almost, as it were, by default.

It must be pointed out at the outset, however, that, strictly speaking, Russell never formulated a genuine "philosophy" of language. Though he made linguistic analysis an integral part of his philosophical method, he never devoloped anything approaching a comprehensive theory to explain how language functions and how linguistic analysis should proceed. There are, of course, implicit in his writings, certain basic assumptions and presuppositions regarding language and the way it functions which can be regarded as rudiments of a philosophy of language. But in the sense that Wittgenstein, for instance, did so, Russell did not develop a "theory" (or "theories") of language. For the most part he was content merely to *practice* linguistic analysis and to leave the fundamental assumptions underlying his practice unarticulated and, it would seem, unexamined.

Indeed, even to say that he practiced linguistic analysis is to say something quite vague, something which, unless clarified, is potentially misleading. For though he regarded analysis of language as an indispensable philosophical technique, he did not conceive it – as many present-day philosophers apparently do – as an enterprise which both begins and ends in language and has as its sole purpose the clarification and classification of various types of linguistic forms. Rather, he was convinced that the philosophical significance of language derives from the fact that, through it, one is able to discern the basis structure of the reality language is about.

The concept of "structure" is fundamental for Russell's analytic method, and explicating it as precisely as is feasible at this point will help us to gain a general understanding of his conception of linguistic analysis as a philosophical method. To some extent, no doubt, as a result of his work in logic and philosophy of mathematics – the areas which first aroused his philosophical interest – he tended to concern himself with the "formal" or "structural" aspects of language. But however much, qua logician-mathematician, he may have been interested in formal structure or "logical syntax" for its own sake, he was, qua philosopher, interested in it for another reason. Operating with what may be called a "reference theory" of meaning, he took the meaning of

an expression to be an entity of some kind which the expression designates; [1] consequently he assumed that meaning analysis is essentially
an examination of the various kinds of entities language is about.
Words, he maintained, are meaningful by virtue of the fact that they
stand for something else; therefore, all symbols that have genuine
meaning must denote some kind of entity. It follows that there should
be a correspondence between the (non-syncategorematic) words in a
proposition [2] and elements in the fact (if any) the proposition asserts.
Consequently the proposition and the fact asserted should have a similar structure; they should, that is, have a similar "logical form." It is
logical form in this sense – the common structure that proposition and
fact supposedly share – that is the object of Russell's philosophical
interest, and it is because there is (he believed) this common structure
that analysis of language can be philosophically significant. It assures
us that if we properly analyze propositions we will not only clarify the
language with which we talk about the world, but will also, at the same
time, gain an understanding of what the world itself is fundamentally
like.

For Russell, then, the discovery of the logical forms of propositions
is the philosophical purpose of linguistic analysis. But how is this to be
accomplished? Logical form, in the sense which seemed to him to be
the philosophically relevant one – inherent structure – does not present
itself for immediate discernment in most propositions. Indeed, he came
to feel that propositions of ordinary language, so far from clearly exhibiting their logical forms, disguise them so thoroughly that only pains-
taking analysis will uncover them. This is primarily due to the fact
that they frequently contain expressions which seem to refer to objects
of one type or another but do not actually do so. Thus he believed that
the only way to exhibit logical form is through analyzing and recasting – or, as I prefer to call it, *reconstructing* – various kinds of propositions of ordinary language in such a way that the non-referential
expressions would be eliminated. The systematic reconstruction of propositions would result in a "logically perfect language," a language,
that is, that would "show at a glance the logical structure of the facts

---

[1] This is not quite accurate. Some words, e.g., articles, prepositions, and conjunctions are
"syncategorematic" and have a type of meaning even though they do not refer.

[2] Russell's use of "proposition" varies. In some of his earliest writings he tended to think of
a proposition as something extra-linguistic which sentences "express." In later writings, however, he takes a proposition to be simply a sentence in the indicative. I shall use it in this latter sense and shall regard it as synonymous with "sentence" and "statement."

asserted or denied." [1] Such a language would represent the theoretical goal of reconstructionism [2] and would stand as the ultimate philosophical accomplishment of linguistic analysis.

It is almost certainly this notion of reconstructionism as the analytic tool needed to effect philosophical clarification of language that is Russell's most important contribution to the linguistic philosophy. The great influence of this method on the early Wittgenstein and the Vienna Circle is a matter of record, and this influence continues to be seen in the work of many present-day philosophers and philosopher-logicians, of whom the most prominent is perhaps Quine. In the last two or three decades, however, Russell's influence in general, and that of his doctrine of reconstructionism in particular, have, in certain philosophical circles at least, definitely declined. A large body of philosophers now feel that the attempt to reconstruct ordinary language is philosophically misguided, that the notion that ordinary language even needs reconstructing manifests a fundamental confusion regarding either the nature of language or the nature of philosophy itself. Especially anathema to these philosophers is the motion of the "ideal" language which is supposed to represent the ultimate goal of reconstructionism. It is, they feel, something of a formalistic artifice which, even if it could be constructed, would be philosophically otiose.

It seems to me, however, that though many of the arguments directed against Russell's attempt to reconstruct ordinary language make legitimate points, many reflect either a failure to see precisely what he hoped to accomplish by means of such reconstruction, or they reflect an inadequate appreciation of the philosophical issues his reconstructionism involves. I shall, therefore, attempt to clarify the nature and

---

[1] "The Philosophy of Logical Atomism," *Monist*, XXVIII (1918), 495–527; XXIX (1919), 32–63, 190–222, 345–380. These essays have been reprinted in Bertrand Russell, *Logic and Knowledge, Essays 1901–1950*; edited by Robert C. Marsh, (London, 1956), pp. 175–282. The present quotation is found on page 198 of the latter. Throughout this study I shall, when referring to these essays, employ the pagination of the 1956 reprint. Subsequently I shall abbreviate the former as *P.L.A.* and the latter as *L.K.* For convenience, I shall also employ a number of other abbreviations when referring to Russell's works. These are as follows: *I.M.P.* (*Introduction to Mathematical Philosophy*), *M.L.* (*Mysticism and Logic*), *O.K.E.W.* (*Our Knowledge of the External World*), *P.B.R.* (*The Philosophy of Bertrand Russell*, Schilpp, ed.), *M.P.D.* (*My Philosophical Development*), *P.M.* (*Principia Mathematica*), *P. of M.* (*The Principles of Mathematics*), *P.P.* (*The Problems of Philosophy*).

[2] I shall refer in this way to the various attempts by Russell to re-cast propositions of ordinary language. I shall also refer, at times, to his "reconstructionist program." Both of these expressions are somewhat misleading in that they suggest that his approach to the reconstruction of language was rather more systematic than it actually was. However, since I shall maintain, throughout this study, that his distinctive analytic method was this kind of reconstructionism of language, it will be convenient to have expressions which will serve to designate, collectively, the different instances of his use of this method.

function of reconstructionism in order to show the significance of the basic philosophical questions it raises. In this way I hope to provide a basis for a proper adjudication of its value as a philosophical method.

Before concluding this introductory section it is necessary to make two clarificatory remarks concerning the scope and character of my examination of Russell's philosophy of language. In the first place, I shall confine my attention to his *early* philosophy, by which I understand that phase of his philosophy culminating in *The Philosophy of Logical Atomism* (1918–19).[1] It was in his early philosophy that he developed and made most extensive and systematic use of his reconstructionist method; therefore a study of this method as it functioned in his early philosophy will permit us to uncover the essential features of reconstructionism and the fundamental assumptions on which it rests. Secondly, my examination of Russell will be "structural" or "thematic" rather than "historical" or "genetic." Throughout this study my aim will be to disclose the "architectonic" features of Russell's philosophy of language. Accordingly, I shall concern myself with the *pervasive* trends in his thought and relate his reconstructionism – and the ancillary doctrines it involves – to these rather than to other views that may also have influenced his thinking on specific points. Moreover, whenever I have occasion to deal with particular features of his philosophy I shall in all cases relate these to his general analytic method (reconstructionism) rather than attempt to place them in the precise context in which they may have had their genesis. This means that the analyses I shall provide of certain developments in his philosophy will emphasize the respects in which they fit into the general pattern of his reconstructionism; I shall not attempt to present an historically adequate account of their significance in Russell's overall philosophical development.

Briefly stated my aim is fourfold: (1) to focus attention on the basic similarities between ostensibly rather different analytic techniques employed by Russell in a variety of contexts to resolve specific philosophical problems; (2) to indicate how, at bottom, they represent an abiding concern to reconstruct language in order to get at its logical structure and, through this, at the ontological structure of reality; (3) to lay

---

[1] Only three works by Russell written subsequent to 1919 will be used in this study. One is the essay, "Logical Atomism," included in J. H. Muirhead, ed., *Contemporary British Philosophy: Personal Statements*, First Series, (London, 1924). (This essay has been reprinted in *L.K.*, pp. 321–342.) The second is "My Mental Development" and "Reply to Critics" in Paul A. Schilpp (ed.), *The Philosophy of Bertrand Russell* (Evanston and Chicago, 1944). The third is his philosophical autobiography, *My Philosophical Development* (London, 1959). All of these are used for the light they shed on his early philosophy.

bare the chief assumptions giving rise to his use of reconstructionism as a philosophical method; and (4) to provide a critique of reconstructionism and the assumptions on which it rests. I shall begin by attempting to clarify what it means to say that, for Russell, the philosophical purpose of linguistic analysis is the elucidation of logical forms.

CHAPTER I

THE QUEST FOR LOGICAL FORM

REFERENCE AND MEANING

In order to understand precisely what is involved in the notion of "logical form" as that concept functions in Russell's philosophy, it will be necessary, first of all, to see the close connection between this concept and the "reference theory" of meaning. This theory played a fundamental role in his conception of linguistic analysis as a philosophical method, and it must be understood if we are to see the intimate relationship he saw between the logical forms of propositions and the ontological forms of facts.

So far as historical influence is concerned, Russell's adoption of a reference theory of meaning seems to have resulted, in part at least, from his early acquaintance with Mill's *Logic*. The influence of Mill on philosophers of the late nineteenth and early twentieth centuries was, in general, very great,[1] and was especially strong perhaps in the case of Russell, for whom the *Logic* served as something of an introduction to serious philosophical literature.[2] And like many other philosophers of the period, Russell tended to follow Mill in focusing attention on what may be called the "naming" function of language. For Mill, *names* and *naming* occupy a central place in logical theory. He says, for instance, that a proposition is formed "by putting together two names";[3] specifically, "every proposition affirms or denies one of these names of the other."[4] Moreover, the basic distinction he makes in classifying differ-

---

[1] Cf. Gilbert Ryle, "The Theory of Meaning," included in C. A. Mace (ed.), *British Philosophy in the Mid-Century* (London, 1957), p. 241: "... it is difficult to exaggerate the influence which he [Mill] exercised, for good and ill, upon British and Continental philosophers.... In particular, Mill's theory of meaning set the questions, and, in large measure, determined the answers for thinkers as different as Brentano, ... Meinong and Husserl; Bradley, Jevons, Frege, James, Peirce, Moore and Russell."

[2] See *M.P.D.*, p. 28.

[3] J. S. Mill, *A System of Logic* (London, 1936), p. 12. All references to Mill will be to this work.

[4] p. 13.

ent types of words is between those that are names and those that are
not. (These latter, which include words like "of," "and," "to," and so
forth, he calls *syncategorematic* words – words which acquire meaning
only in context. All nouns and adjectives he treats as "context-free"
names.) And finally, his theory of meaning requires that in all propositions in which something is being genuinely predicated of a subject – as
distinguished from those cases in which the subject is merely being defined – the existence of some object named by the subject-term is implied. *Something* must be named even in those propositions where the
subject-term would normally be considered to be vacuous, as in the case
of (to use Mill's example), "The ghost of a murdered person haunts the
couch of the murderer." This proposition, he maintains, "can only have
meaning if understood as implying a belief in ghosts; for since the signification of the word 'ghost' implies nothing [really existing,] ... the
speaker either means nothing, or means to assert a thing which he
wishes to be believed to have really taken place." [1] That is to say, unless the existence of the referent of the word "ghost" is assumed, the
sentence is meaningless, for (the subject-term being vacuous) nothing
has been asserted. For Mill, then, the paradigm for meaning is naming,
and his whole analysis of the way linguistic expressions function is conditioned by this fact.

The influence of Mill's logical theory is immediately evident in certain passages of Russell's early treatise, *Principles of Mathematics*. Like
Mill, Russell regarded the *nomen-nominatum* relationship as paradig-
matic for all (non-syncategorematic) words, and in his discussion of
"philosophical grammar" in this work [2] he treats adjectives (which he
calls "general names") and verbs as referential in a way analogous to
the way proper names are referential. What a particular adjective or
verb means is, he assumes, to be decided by locating the appropriate
"object" to which it refers. In general, proper names are said to designate *things* whereas adjectives and verbs designate (different kinds of)
concepts. Adjectives designate *predicates* and verbs designate *relations*.
Despite differences in the *kinds* of objects they designate, however, proper names, adjectives, and verbs are alike in that they designate – or
can be used to designate – what Russell calls "terms." [3] In his words,

---

[1] p. 73.

[2] See Vol. I, Chapter V. Second edition, (London, 1937).

[3] Russell's view is somewhat more complex that my presentation here would indicate. *As
such*, neither adjectives nor verbs are said to designate *terms*. Whereas a proper name "when
it occurs in a proposition, is always ... the subject that the proposition ... is about," adjectives and verbs "are capable of occurring in propositions in which they cannot be regarded

"Whatever may be an object of thought, or may occur in any true or false proposition, or can be counted as one, I call a *term*. This, then, is the widest word in the philosophical vocabulary. I shall use as synonymous with it the words unit, individual, and entity. The first two emphasize the fact that every term is *one*, while the third is derived from the fact that every term has being, *i.e.*, *is* in some sense. A man, a moment, a number, a class, a relation, a chimaera, or anything else that can be mentioned, is sure to be a term; and to deny that such and such a thing is a term must always be false." [1] At this time Russell believed that if a word has meaning, there must be an extra-linguistic entity of some sort corresponding to it, and this he believed to be the case whether the word in question were a noun, a verb, or an adjective, and whether the referent in question were a physical object, an abstraction, a fiction, or whatever.

Though he subsequently rejected the extreme form of the reference theory to which he subscribed in *P. of M.*, Russell nevertheless continued to think of meaning in terms of reference. Indicative of this is a passage in *P. L. A.*, where he says, "... the components of a proposition are the symbols we must understand in order to understand the proposition ... the components of the fact which makes a proposition true or false, as the case may be, are the meanings of the symbols which we must understand in order to understand the proposition." [2] According to this conception of meaning, words in sentences designate elements of facts, and these elements are the *meanings* of the words. As I understand Russell, facts are kinds of "complexes" made up of the various objects that are the referents of words in the proposition asserting the fact. Taking the proposition "Caesar crossed the Rubicon" as an example, the fact corresponding to this proposition would be a complex of the referents of the words "Caesar," "the Rubicon," and the relational word "crossed." The import of what Russell is

---

as subject, but only as parts of the assertion." (*Ibid.*) As "parts of the assertion" adjectives and verbs designate concepts, but not concepts *used as terms*. Precisely the same concepts, however, *can* be used as terms if the sentences in which they occur are properly formulated. (Cf. pp. 46, 48) For example, the sentence "Socrates is human" can be re-stated as "humanity belongs to Socrates" (p. 45) and the verb "kills," which in the sentence "Felton killed Buckingham" functions simply as part of the assertion, functions as the subject of the sentence "*kills* does not mean the same as *to kill*." (p. 48) The difference between a "concept as such" and a "concept used as a term" corresponds, then, for Russell, to the *syntactical* difference between adjectives and verbs functioning as such and (transmuted into nouns) functioning as logical subjects of sentences. In both cases, however, they are said to function referentially and to *mean* the concepts to which they refer.

[1] p. 44.
[2] p. 196.

saying in the passage just quoted is, I take it, that if in the case of any of these words there were no "object" of the appropriate type corresponding to it, then that word would not have a meaning. In order to have a meaning a word must stand for some entity; it must, that is, mean some*thing*.

Further evidence of the extent to which Russell's thinking concerning language and linguistic analysis was dominated by a pervasive tendency to equate meaning and reference can be seen in an illuminating passage in *M. P. D.* where he says, "I have never been able to feel any sympathy with those who treat language as an autonomous province. The essential thing about language is that it has meaning – i.e. that it is related to something other than itself, which is, in general, non-linguistic."[1] This passage is particularly significant, I think, since it occurs in a context in which Russell is explicitly *opposing* his own views on language to those incorporated into certain contemporary trends in the linguistic philosophy. Here, then, we see Russell not simply stating, but *insisting on*, the philosophical significance of the referential function of language. And we see also, of course, that he is once again equating *having meaning* with *having reference*.

Many other instances of Russell's assimilation of meaning to reference could be provided, but this, I feel, is unnecessary. Though brief, the preceding discussion of the reference theory as it functioned in Russell's philosophy is sufficient to show that, for him, the basic dimension of language was the semantic dimension and the basic function of language the referring function. This much understood, we are now in a position to examine his concept of "logical form."

TWO SENSES OF "LOGICAL FORM"

The concept of "logical form" is of central importance for Russell's analytic method, so much so that it is hardly an exaggeration to say that, for him, exhibiting the logical forms of propositions is the ultimate purpose of all philosophical analysis of language. As the concept functions in Russell's philosophy of language, however, it cannot be simply and straightforwardly equated, as it usually is, with the general schema of a proposition, discoverable by abstracting from its specific content. There are, I believe, two different, though related, senses in which "form" is involved in Russell's philosophy of language, a "narrow" and a "wide" sense. The latter is, for my purposes, of more im-

[1] p. 14.

portance, since it is more directly related to his distinctive philosophy of language. Before examining it, however, I shall briefly examine the narrow concept in order to prepare for a discussion of logical form in the wide sense.

Since Russell's interest in liguistic analysis as a philosophical method was aroused, orginally, by a desire to resolve certain problems he encountered in symbolic logic and the foundations of mathematics, it is not surprising that his initial approach to analysis of language would be formalistic, emphasizing structural and syntactical features. Thus he did think it important to analyze propositions in terms of the general schema underlying the particular content of a proposition, so that propositions with quite different subject matters can be said to have identical forms. Such propositions as "Socrates is mortal," "Jones is angry", "the sun is hot," etc., diverse as they are with respect to what they are *about*, have, he suggests, something in common, "something indicated by the word 'is.'" [1] This common feature is, of course, their "form," and according to Russell, "It is forms, in this sense, that are the proper object of philosophical logic." [2]

In this sense of "form" the propositions in question can be said to have a common from because in all cases the word "is" is the "is" of predication and expresses the kind of relationship existing between some object and a property ascribed to it. All of these propositions, that is, exemplify the same logical schema, $P_{(s)}$, and this, in the narrow sense, is their logical form. Analysis of propositions into their forms, so conceived, is usually undertaken to facilitate inquiry into their logical relationships. For purposes of formal logic the particular subject-matter or content of a statement is irrelevant; only the abstract form is involved in those inferences which characterize logical deduction.

It is to be noted, however, that even in this narrow sense, the concept of logical form has more than a purely "formal" significance for Russell. Quite early, as a consequence of his study of Leibniz, he came to the conclusion that whole metaphysical systems have resulted from certain far-reaching – and, he believed, erroneous – assumptions regarding the forms of propositions. In *M. P. D.* he recounts how this came about: "I found – what books on Leibniz failed to make clear – that his metaphysic was explicitly based upon the doctrine that every proposition attributed a predicate to a subject and (what seemed to him almost the

---

[1] *Our Knowledge of the External World* (New York, 1960), p. 40. This work is comprised of a series of lectures originally delivered in Boston in 1914.
[2] *Ibid.*, p. 41.

same thing) that every fact consists of a substance having a property. I found that this same doctrine underlies the systems of Spinoza, Hegel, and Bradley, who, in fact, all developed the doctrine with more logical rigour than is shown by Leibniz."[1]

The fact that such monumental edifices could be founded on what he regarded as an untenable assumption concerning forms of propositions suggested to him that perhaps "philosophy had erred in adopting heroic remedies for intellectual difficulties," [2] and it led him to believe that "solutions were to be found merely by greater care and accuracy." [3] In the case in question, the "greater care and accuracy" required is a less prejudiced analysis of the forms of propositions. Such an analysis, he felt, will disclose that it is a gross misrepresentation of linguistic forms to regard them all as reducible to the subject-predicate form. Many propositions, he insisted, are irreducibly *relational*, and we cannot, without distorting their true forms, interpret them as anything else. Considering the proposition, "This thing is bigger than that," for instance, he argues, "If we say 'this thing is bigger than that,' we are not assigning a mere quality of 'this,' but a relation of 'this' and 'that.' We might express the same fact by saying that 'that thing is smaller than this,' where grammatically the subject is changed. Thus propositions stating that two things have a certain relation have a different form from subject-predicate propositions, and the failure to perceive this difference or to allow for it has been the source of many errors in traditional metaphysics." [4]

As a result of these considerations he came to feel that it is essential, when engaged in philosophical analysis, to determine the true logical forms of the propositions being analyzed, in order to avoid forcing them into some pre-determined form, such as the subject-predicate schema. To fail to do so is to risk being led astray, by inadequate analysis of language, into a metaphysical theory which misleads us vis-à-vis the true nature of reality. In his essay, "Logical Atomism," he expresses this point in the following way: "The influence of language on philo-

---

[1] p. 61.
[2] "Logical Atomism," *L.K.*, p. 324.
[3] *Ibid.*
[4] *O.K.E.W.*, p. 42. This is a later, very summary statement of his critique of the subject-predicate logic, formulated originally and much more extensively in *P. of M.* The objections Russell provides in the earlier work are too elaborate to permit intelligible paraphrase or succinct quotation. In that work (see pp. 221–226) he analyzes both the "monadistic" and "monistic" versions of the view that "no relations can possess absolute and metaphysical validity," (p. 221) and shows that neither version can adequately deal with asymmetrical relations. The embarrassment asymmetrical relations occasion for the subject-predicate logic is also treated, briefly, in *O.K.E.W.*, pp. 44ff.

sophy has, I believe, been profound and almost unrecognized. If we are not to be misled by this influence, it is necessary to become conscious of it, and ask ourselves deliberately how far it is legitimate. The subject-predicate logic, with the substance-attribute metaphysic, are a case in point .... We must be on our guard ... if our logic is not to lead to a false metaphysic." [1] And a little later, discussing the influence of syntax on philosophical theories, he says: "Almost any proposition can be put into a form in which it has a subject and predicate, united by a copula. It is natural to infer that every fact has a corresponding form, and consists in the possession of a quality by a substance. This leads, of course, to monism, since the fact that there were several substances (if it were a fact) would not have the requisite form. Philosophers, as a rule, believe themselves free from this sort of influence of linguistic forms, but most of them seem to me to be mistaken in this belief." [2] From these passages it is clear that analysis of linguistic forms was, for Russell, no mere formal exercise, undertaken for the purpose of exhibiting interesting features of logical syntax. The forms of propositions have a metaphysical significance, and correct analysis of certain kinds of propositions can illumine the structure of the reality corresponding to them.

Despite the considerable philosophical significance of logical form in the sense I have been discussing, it is, nonetheless, a sense which is restricted to *syntactical* features of propositions, to those features, that is, which represent the way in which the constituents of a proposition are related. It is logical form in this sense to which Russell is referring when he says, "In every proposition there is, besides the particular subject-matter concerned, a certain *form*, a way in which the constituents of the proposition ... are put together." [3] Following a distinction of which he makes use in "Logical Atomism," we may say that, so conceived, logical form involves *syntax* but not *vocabulary*.[4]

What this means can be seen by considering a simple example, the proposition, "Socrates loves Plato." According to Russell, "traditional logic," which recognized only one form of (non-complex) proposition, the subject-predicate form, would require that this proposition be in-

---

[1] *L.K.*, pp. 330–1.
[2] *Ibid.*, p. 331.
[3] *O.K.E.W.*, p. 40.
[4] Cf. *L.K.*, p. 331: "... language misleads us both by its vocabularly and its syntax.... Syntax and vocabulary have different kinds of effects on philosophy. Vocabulary has most influence on common sense.... common sense is influenced by the existence of [a] word, and tends to suppose that one word must stand for one object...."

terpreted in some such way as "Socrates is a lover of Plato," in order to exhibit its "true" structure and show that it really ascribes a predicate to Socrates, viz., the property of *being a lover of Plato*. As we have seen, he believed that interpreting a proposition in this way, in order to make it conform to a pre-conceived notion as to what propositional forms *must* be, is misleading and philosophically unjustified. If we approach analysis of language without such a bias, we will see that, in the case in question, the proposition is not a subject-predicate proposition at all, but a relational one, with "loves" designating a relation between the two constituents Socrates and Plato.

The point to which I wish to call attention here is that so long as Russel is concerned to exhibit logical form in the sense we are now considering (the "narrow" sense), the kind of analysis he employs does not involve an investigation of the status of the constituents and hence does not extend to the domain of "vocabulary." On both the aforementioned interpretations of "Socrates loves Plato," it is assumed that "Socrates" and "Plato" function as names and refer to genuine elements in the fact which the proposition asserts. (Even on the interpretation to which Russell is opposed – in which Plato is regarded as merely an element in the predicate ascribed to Socrates, rather than, as he believes, a term of a relation – "Plato" is still regarded as functioning as a name, designating an entity taken as ontologically basic.) In such cases as this, then, the only issue is the correct way to analyze the proposition so as to exhibit *the relationship between the constituents*. The status of the words (ostensibly) standing for constituents, and therefore (ostensibly) designating ontologically basic entities in the corresponding fact is not called into question.

It is because logical form as I have considered it thus far does not encompass the *constituents* of propositions that I have referred to it as logical form in the *narrow* sense. And it is this sense, it seems, which Russell usually has in mind when he explicitly refers to the "form" or "logical form" of a proposition. In an extended sense, however, the concept of "logical form" can be said to be involved in his analyses of propositions which do include an examination of the constituents. It will be my immediate task to show the function which this wider concept of form has in his philosophy of language and to delineate the way in which it involves propositional constituents.

The most convenient way to approach these questions is to reconsider the relationship which, according to Russell, holds between propositions and facts. It was his view that between them there is a more or less strict *isomorphism*, so that facts can not only be said to have a form, but precisely the *same* form as the propositions which assert them. Indeed, for the most part he seems not to have regarded it as necessary even to argue this point; usually he simply took it for granted, as in the following passage: "Two facts are said to have the same 'form' when they differ only as regards their constituents. In this case, we may suppose the one to result from the other by *substitution* of different constituents. For example, 'Napoleon hates Wellington' results from 'Socrates loves Plato' by substituting Napoleon for Socrates, Wellington for Plato, and *hates* for *loves*. It is obvious that some, but not all, facts can be thus derived from 'Socrates loves Plato.' Thus some facts have the same form as this and some have not. We can represent the form of a fact by the use of variables: thus 'xRy' may be used to represent the form of the fact that Socrates loves Plato." [1] Here, patently, the forms in question are *directly* forms of the *propositions*, "Napoleon hates Wellington" and "Socrates loves Plato." But since, on the assumption that proposition and fact are isomorphic, they are also forms of *facts* corresponding to these propositions, Russell does not think it necessary to mention the forms of the propositions (as such) at all, but assumes that he may refer straightforwardly to the forms of the facts. It follows on the isomorphic-assumption that we will, if we properly analyze a proposition, effect an analysis of the fact corresponding to it as well. The proposition is said to "mirror" [2] the fact in such a way that we may discern the form of the fact by discovering the form of the proposition in which that fact is reflected.

Generally speaking, then, if we are to discover the true form of the fact, we must determine the form of the proposition corresponding to it. In order to accomplish this, however, it is not sufficient, as Russel became increasingly aware, to confine ourselves to an investigation of syntax; in addition, it is necessary to examine the status of the putative constituents of the proposition. Not, of course, that he ever, at any time, underestimated the importance of knowing what the true constituents of a proposition are. The significant difference in his changing concepti on of the role played by constituents in determining the "form" of a proposition represents, rather, a complication of his initial view as to how this form is to be discovered. Of fundamental importance, in con-

---

[1] "On Propositions: What They Are and How They Mean," *Proceedings of the Aristotelian Society*, Sup. v. II (1919). This essay has been reprinted in *L.K.*, pp. 283–320. The above passage is found on page 286 of the latter.

[2] Cf. *P.L.A.*, p. 197: "... there is an objective complexity in the world and ... it is mirrored by the complexity of propositions."

nection with this point, was his discovery, as a result of the theory of descriptions, that some words and phrases which seem to function as constituents of propositions can not be, ultimately, regarded as such. This being the case, analysis must expose these expressions for what they are and *reconstruct* propositions in which they occur in such a way that, not they, but the real constituents of the proposition become evident. In this way the form the proposition assumes, clarified with respect to both syntax *and* vocabulary, will be exhibited.

It is this more comprehensive conception of form – one which takes cognizance of the way the structure of a proposition is affected by the status of the symbols ostensibly functioning as constituents – that I call logical from in the "wide" sense. And though, as I have suggested, Russell rarely explicitly refers to logical form in this sense, it is clear that many of his attempts to reconstruct propositions aim at showing that the proposition being reconstructed has, due to the presence of symbols which purport to function as genuine constituents, but do not, a faulty *structure*, a form which is different from the form of the fact corresponding to the proposition. Consider, for example, this passage from *P. L. A.*: "The word 'Picadilly' will form part of many significant propositions, but the facts corresponding to these propositions do not contain any single constituent, whether simple or complex, corresponding to the word 'Picadilly.' That is to say, if you take language as a guide in your analysis of the fact expressed, you will be led astray in a statement of that sort." [1] Here Russell is calling attention to the way the presence of the word "Picadilly" in propositions misleads us concerning the forms of the facts corresponding to them, since there is no such constituent to be found in these facts. So long as he did not question the status of the constituent-symbols, so long, that is, as he took them at their grammatical "face value," as symbols for genuine constituents, he naturally assumed these as the fundamental elements in the propositions in which they occurred. When he came to question their status, however, he saw that it was necessary to take account of how this status affects determination of the overall structure of the proposition and of the fact it asserts or denies.

This point can be considerably elucidated, I think, by a brief exegesis of the developments in Russell's thought that led him to reject unreconstructed grammatical form as a reliable guide to logical form. Early, in *P. of M.*, he seems to have felt that grammatical form is a fairly reliable index of logical form, and he suggests there that in ana-

[1] p. 191.

lyzing language "grammar ... though not our master, ... be taken as our guide." [1] Here, indeed, it was part of his task to *defend* ordinary grammar against claims of philosophers such as Bradley who would, he claimed, misrepresent it for their own purposes. Consequently he believed that "Although a grammatical distinction cannot be uncritically assumed to correspond to a genuine philosophical difference," still, "on the whole grammar seems ... to bring us much nearer to a correct logic than the current opinions of philosophers."[2] Various considerations, however, gradually led him to conclude that as an indicator of the true forms of propositions, ordinary grammar is at least as misleading as it is illuminating. More and more he moved toward the view to which he gives utterance in his "Reply to Criticisms,"[3] that "obstinate addiction to ordinary language ... is one of the main obstacles to progress in philosophy."

Though there were undoubtedly other factors which contributed to the distrust he came to have in the philosophical adequacy of ordinary language, it would appear that it was primarily due to his growing belief that ordinary language is defective in the way it misleads us regarding the *true constituents* of propositions. I mentioned just now, in passing, that Russell's analysis of descriptive phrases was responsible for awakening him to the realization that some words which seem to function as constituents of propositions do not actually do so. As he himself has put it, "[this analysis] led me to pay attention to the problem of meaning and significance."[4] More specifically, it helped him to realize that "in analysing a significant sentence, one must not assume that each separate word or phrase has significance on its own account." [5] As we have seen, before he came to this realization, his adoption of a thoroughgoing reference theory of meaning had led him, in *P. of M.*, to an exaggerated kind of realism, with an entity of some sort corresponding to virtually every type of linguistic expression. His analysis of descriptive phrases, then, represents a major turning point in his philosophy of language in general and his conception of logical structure in particular, for it led him to place important limitations on the linguistic expressions which can be said to function referentially.

It will be helpful to consider, at this point, the kind of significance the theory of descriptions had for his philosophy of language, and to

---

[1] p. 42.
[2] *Ibid.*
[3] *P.B.R.*, p. 694.
[4] "My Mental Development," *Ibid.*, p. 14.
[5] *Ibid.*

show how, from this, he went on to question the status of other types of putative constituent-symbols. I shall, accordingly, sketch here the general pattern of his analysis of descriptive phrases and then, very briefly, relate this to his analyses of two other important kinds of symbols – class-symbols and physical-object symbols. Since my aim here is simply to clarify as much as possible the question of how the concept of logical form (in the wide sense) involves propositional constituents, I shall not investigate at this time any of the numerous important philosophical issues connected with these analyses.[1]

LOGICAL FORM, PROPOSITIONAL CONSTITUENTS, AND RECONSTRUCTIONISM

In the early part of this century, many philosophers, under the influence of Mill's *Logic* (including, of course, Russell), had assumed that descriptions, particularly definite descriptions, function as names.[2] Such phrases were frequently called "compound" or "complex" names to indicate both their grammatical difference from, and logical similarity to, ordinary names. Interpreted as names, they would, of course, be genuine constituents in the propositions in which they occur, and these propositions would be *about* the entities they supposedly designate. For reasons which I shall explain in the next chapter, Russell thought it important to show that despite their grammatical similarity to propositions containing proper names, propositions containing descriptive phrases have a quite different logical structure. Making use of the analytic machinery provided by the new mathematical logic, he was able to show that when translated into its true (logical) form, a proposition of this type does not contain, as a constituent, either the descriptive phrase itself or any equivalent expression. He did this through interpreting such propositions as general (existential) propositions concerning properties prossessed by some unique individual, rather than – as they seem, prima facie, to be – singular statements *about* the individual.

According to this interpretation descriptive phrases are said to be "incomplete symbols," symbols "that have absolutely no meaning whatsoever in isolation but merely acquire a meaning in context." [3]

---

[1] The instances of reconstructionism discussed briefly in the following sections will be treated in considerably more detail in Chapter II.

[2] Throughout this discussion and the discussion in the following chapter, what I have to say concerning descriptions should be understood as applying only to *definite* descriptions.

[3] *P.L.A.*, p. 253.

For the present it will be sufficient to explicate the meaning of what Russell is saying here by pointing out that, for him, to have meaning "in isolation" is to refer to some entity. This is not to say simply that there must be some entity corresponding to the expression said to have meaning "in isolation"; this is not, I think, Russell's point, or at least not the whole of his point. The question at issue here is the logical function of the expression, how it acquires its meaning. There are, of course, entities corresponding to many descriptive phrases: indeed, any name can be transformed into a descriptive phrase simply by using the name as a constant to replace the variable in the expression "the thing called x." Nonetheless, a descriptive phrase *as such* does not, according to Russell, have a referential function and therefore is an incomplete symbol. What meaning it has it derives from the fact that it can be a fragment of a meaningful proposition. In this respect it is much like an ordinary syncategorematic word, and can be no more a genuine constituent of a proposition than can the latter.

In analyzing descriptive phrases as incomplete symbols, Russell believed he had succeeded in showing how we may attribute meaning to propositions in which such phrases occur without assuming that these propositions are *about* their referents in the sense that a proposition having a proper name as subject is about the nominatum of that name. This enabled him to dispense with entities presumed to serve as the nominata of descriptions on the assumption that these too function as names. From the point of view of what it shows about logical, as opposed to grammatical, form, there are two ways of looking at what Russell's analysis of descriptions accomplishes. On the one hand, we may say that it brings our symbolism more into line with the structure of facts, since, clarified in accordance with this analysis, propositions containing descriptive phrases no longer appear to contain phrases to which nothing corresponds in the facts these propositions assert. On the other hand, we may say that, as a result of the analysis, we have gained insight into the structure of facts, since we now see that facts corresponding to propositions containing descriptive phrases do not have the kind of form they were thought to have when it was assumed that such propositions are singular statements about individuals. In either case, we have made an important advance in our investigation of logical form, and it is perhaps only a matter of emphasis whether we say that the kind of progress involved is more *logical* or *ontological.*

Russell's theory of descriptions was first formulated in his essay,

"On Denoting" (1905). Shortly thereafter, in *Principia Mathematica*,[1] he made use of a similar kind of analysis in his investigation of class-symbols. In his investigation of classes in *P. of M.* (1903), he had encountered several problems occasioned by his assumption there that classes are entities denoted by class-symbols. To mention but one of these, there was the problem of whether a class is more appropriately characterized in terms of the concept that determines the class (the intensional interpretation), or in terms of the members that make up the class (the extensional interpretation). A decision on this question is vital for any theory that accords a referential function to class-symbols, since, assuming one interpretation, a class will be a *unity* and, assuming the other, a *plurality*; or, as Russell expressed it, it will be a "one" or a "many." In *P. M.*, with the theory of descriptions as a model, he provided an analysis that he believed enabled him to resolve this and other problems, by showing that they need not arise at all. Class-symbols, he suggested, are also incomplete symbols and are no more constituents of propositions than are descriptive phrases. In order to avoid confusion about the logical forms of propositions containing such symbols, then, these propositions must be reconstructed in such a way that symbols ostensibly designating classes can be eliminated. This can be accomplished, he maintained, by interpreting all sentences concerning classes as sentences involving properties and the individuals that possess these properties. As in the case of descriptions, this kind of interpretation will permit us to attribute meaning to propositions about classes without postulating entities to serve as the referents of class-symbols.

A third important type of constituent-symbol Russell called into question (several years later) [2] was physical object symbols. Here too his inquiry into the status of these symbols was occasioned by a problem resulting from the fact that in ordinary language they are presumed to be genuine constituents of propositions. Primarily for epistemological reasons – which I shall examine at a later time – he came to believe that the ordinary way of conceiving physical objects is philosophically inadequate and should be replaced by a conception of physical objects as "constructions" out of sense-data. Though he nowhere calls physical-

---

[1] With A. N. Whitehead (Cambridge, England, 1910), Vol. I, pp. 71–81.

[2] In *O.K.E.W.*, chapters III and IV and in two essays: "The Ultimate Constituents of Matter," *Monist*, XXV (July, 1915), pp. 399–417; and "The Relation of Sense-data to Physics," *Scientia*, No. 4, 1914. The two essays were subsequently included as chapters VII and VIII of *Mysticism and Logic* (1918). When I shall have occasion to refer to the two essays, I shall employ the pagination of a later edition (New York, 1957) of *M.L.*

object symbols "incomplete symbols," it is clear that his analysis of these symbols aims at accomplishing the same kind of thing that the earlier analyses try to accomplish, i.e., it tries to show that they do not function referentially and therefore are not constituents of the propositions in which they occur. Rather, their presence in sentences indicates that something is being asserted about series or sets of sense-data. Consequently, statements containing physical-object symbols incorrectly mirror the facts they assert and give a false picture of the logical form of both proposition and fact.

On the basis of this extremely brief sketch of three instances in which Russell found ordinary language inadequate in its capacity to convey logical form, it is possible, I think, to see how logical form, in the extended sense, involves propositional constituents. Despite certain differences, his analyses of descriptions, class-symbols, and physical-object symbols all show how the presence of the symbol or phrase in a proposition misrepresents its true form. It does so because it suggests that there is, corresponding to the expression, an entity of some kind that is a constituent of any fact the proposition may assert. However, since the expression is not genuinely referential, no fact which may be asserted by the proposition would contain, as a constituent, an entity corresponding to the expression. Thus the isomorphism between proposition and fact does not obtain, and the true form of the proposition is concealed. It is the task of reconstructionism to remedy this defect by recasting the proposition in such a way that its true form is explicated. When this is accomplished the isomorphic relationship between proposition and fact will be established, and the real constituents of both will become evident.

THE "LOGICALLY PERFECT" LANGUAGE

Systematically pursued, the clarification of logical form effected through reconstructionism would theoretically culminate in an "ideal" or "logically perfect" language. In such a language, Russell says, "there will always be a certain fundamental identity of structure between a fact and the symbol for it ...." [1] What he means by "a certain fundamental identity of structure" is made clear in the following passage: "In a logically perfect language, there will be one word and no more for every simple object, and anything that is not simple will be expressed by a combination of words, by a combination derived, of course, from

[1] *P.L.A.*, p. 197.

the words for the simple things that enter in, one word for each simple component. A language of that sort will be completely analytic, and will show at a glance the logical structure of the facts asserted or denied." [1] Patently, this is not the case where ordinary language is concerned. As noted above, ordinary language is, Russell believed, conspicuously deficient in its capacity to "show at a glance the logical structure of the facts asserted or denied," and it is because it is deficient in this way that reconstructionism is philosophically requisite. This is, of course, only a *philosophical* requirement; for ordinary purposes ordinary language is quite adequate. Indeed, he insists, "Actual languages ... cannot possibly be [logically perfect] if they are to serve the purposes of ordinary life." [2] For philosophical purposes, however, it is necessary to reconstruct ordinary language so that its fundamental structure becomes evident.

In the quest for a logically perfect language, what is sought is the logical form of the *basic propositions* which constitute the bed-rock of the whole linguistic superstructure. These basic propositions Russell designated *atomic* propositions, and each such proposition is said to assert directly some *atomic fact*. It is, of course, because they assert atomic facts that they can be considered the foundational elements of the whole language. Being the "simplest sort of fact" [3] atomic facts have a special status in the hierarchy of facts; [4] consequently, propositions which assert (or "mirror") them will have a special significance, for their constituent-words will directly designate the ontologically basic elements which go to make up such facts.

If we adopt Russell's suggestion to regard qualities as "monadic relations," we may say that "all atomic propositions assert relations of various orders," [5] ranging from propositions which attribute a quality to some object (e.g., "This is white") to those which assert dyadic relations ("This is to the left of that"), triadic relations ("A gives B to C"), and so on. This means that the facts which atomic propositions assert can be said to be made up entirely of *terms* – designated "particulars" – and relations. Together particulars and relations make up the "simple

---

[1] *Ibid.*, pp. 197–198.
[2] *Ibid.*, p. 198.
[3] *Ibid.*
[4] An atomic proposition Russell defines as "A proposition ... which, when asserted, asserts that a certain thing has a certain quality, or that certain things have a certain relation ...." (*O.K.E.W.*, p. 48) Such propositions are of special significance in that they are also the *basic* propositions, in the sense that facts corresponding to them have as constituents the ultimate elements which make up the world.
[5] *Ibid.*, p. 199.

objects" mentioned above which the words in an ideal language would designate. Among these two types of simples, it is the former that receive by far the greater share of Russell's attention. Words for relations – including qualities – he takes at face value as referring to ultimate simples. However, in order to discover the true particulars and the words that stand for them, rigorous analysis is required. For this reason the present discussion will be concerned exclusively with Russell's search for particulars and particular-words.

Russell seems to have regarded it as axiomatic that there are such ultimate simples as particulars are supposed to be, but it is not completely clear just why he thought their existence must be assumed. Some light is shed on this question, however, by his statement that "the definition of a particular is something purely logical" and the following elucidatory remarks: "The question whether this or that is a particular, is a question to be decided in terms of that logical definition. In order to understand the definition it is not necessary to know beforehand 'This is a particular' or 'That is a particular.' It remains to be investigated what particulars you find in the world, if any. The whole question of what particulars you find in the real world is a purely empirical one which does not interest the logician as such." [1] Also serving to illuminate the question before us is a passage from his Introduction to Wittgenstein's *Tractatus*: "If an atomic fact is analysed as fully as possible (theoretical, not practical possibility is meant) the constituents finally reached may be called 'simples' or 'objects.' It is not contended . . . that we can actually isolate the simple or have empirical knowledge of it. It is a logical necessity demanded by theory, like an electron." [2] Taken together, these passages suggest two important points: (1) particulars are not simply *postulated* in order to satisfy some requirement stemming from the metaphysical doctrine associated with logical atomism; (2) qua logical "simple," it is not an essential characteristic of a particular that it be empirically accessible. These points must be examined.

---

[1] *Ibid.*

[2] L. Wittgenstein, *Tractatus Logico-Philosophicus* (London, 1922), p. 12. Here Russell is, of course, discussing Wittgenstein's theory of "simples," not, directly at any rate, his own theory. It seems clear, however, that, under the influence of Wittgenstein, Russell accepted a quite similar view of atomic facts and of "simples." He *did* believe it possible to "isolate the simple" and to "have empirical knowledge of it," for he identified particulars with sense-data. This, however, is a further question; it is, following his own distinction, a "purely empirical question," not a "logical" one. The question we are considering now is the logical status of particulars, and on this point Russell seems to have agreed with Wittgenstein that a particular is a "logical necessity."

Concerning the first point it may be said that it is true, of course, that Russell's logical atomism imvolves, besides a method of analysis, a metaphysical view of the world as composed of entities such as particulars are supposed to be.[1] But he does not seem to have thought it merely a question of postulating such entities. Like Wittgenstein, he seems to have believed that, in the last analysis, language *presupposes* particulars, logically requires them. In their absence our words simply would not have, as he believes they must have, a "definite and unique meaning." Elsewhere in his Introduction to the *Tractatus* he says, "logic has two problems to deal with in regard to Symbolism: (1) the conditions for sense rather than nonsense in combinations of symbols; (2) the conditions for uniqueness of meaning or reference in symbols or combinations of symbols. A logically perfect language has rules of syntax which prevent nonsense, and has single symbols which always have a definite and unique meaning." [2] Here the influence of the reference theory on Russell's thinking comes once again into clear focus. Since the basic words in a language must have a "definite and unique meaning," it follows, according to this theory, that there must be absolutely simple entities functioning as the "meanings" of these words. According to the reference theory, if there were no entities at all corresponding to these basic words, nothing for them to refer to, they would be totally without meaning; and if these entities were not *simple* (non-complex) entities, they would not provide *definite, unique* meanings. Thus, the terms of an atomic fact must be simple, since, if the terms of a fact are not simple, that fact is, by definition, not atomic – it can be further analyzed into facts containing as constituents the simple elements which the basic terms designate. It is to be noted that, in itself, this requirement does not dictate that any particular *kind* of object be taken as "simple," only that whatever kind of object is taken as basic, it must, within the language-system, *function* as simple. It may be that certain kinds of objects are inherently better qualified for this than others – some, of course, are more obviously "complex" than are others – but that is another matter. In sum: there must be atomic facts because there must be something for the basic propositions of a language to assert; and these must be made up of particulars (together with vari-

---

[1] In the last of the lectures included in *P.L.A.*, entitled "Excursus into Metaphysics: What There Is," we find the following statement: "One purpose that has run through all that I have said has been the justification of analysis, i.e., the justification of logical atomism, of the view that you can get down in theory, if not in practice, to ultimate simples, out of which the world is built, and that these simples have a kind of reality not belonging to anything else." (p. 270).

[2] *Tractatus*, "Introduction," p. 8.

ous types of relations) because there must be simple entities to serve as the "meanings" of the basic words.

So conceived, then – and this brings us to the second point – particulars need not be identified with entities whose empirical accessibility affords them an epistemically privileged status. It is important to realize this because Russell, despite his insistence that "the definition of a particular is something purely logical," does not clearly distinguish between particulars *qua terms of relations in atomic facts* and particulars *qua objects of immediate awareness in sense experience.* And it is his assimilation of one conception of particular to the other which leads him to conclude that, insofar as they function as referents of logically basic words – words, that is, that would appear in a logically perfect language – only entities of which we are immediately aware (entities with which we are, as he says, "acquainted") can be regarded as particulars. Thus, he maintains that "A name ... in the narrow logical sense of a word whose meaning is a particular, can only be applied to a particular with which the speaker is acquainted, because you cannot name anything you are not acquainted with." [1] In order to show how he arrived at this conclusion it will be necessary to discuss in some detail his theory of acquaintance.

THE THEORY OF ACQUAINTANCE

As early as 1905, in his essay, "On Denoting," Russell distinguished two forms of knowledge: "acquaintance" and "knowledge about." The distinction between them is "the distinction between the things we have presentations of, and the things we only reach by means of denoting phrases." [2] In this essay his remarks concerning these two different kinds of knowledge are quite brief and are somewhat obscure due to the fact that he is discussing them in the context of a rather intricate analysis of denoting phrases. In his concluding remarks, however, he says, "when there is anything with which we do not have immediate acquaintance, but only definition by denoting phrases, then the propositions in which this thing is introduced by means of denoting phrases do not really contain this thing as a constituent, but contain instead the constituents expressed by the several words of the denoting phrase. Thus in every proposition that we can apprehend ... all the

---

[1] *P.L.A.*, p. 201.

[2] "On Denoting" originally appeared in *Mind*, XIV, pp. 479–493. It has been reprinted in *L.K.*, pp. 39–56. All page references to this essay will refer to the pagination of *L.K.* The present passage is found on p. 41.

constituents are really entities with which we have immediate acquaintance." [1] This passage clearly relates the epistemological concept
"acquaintance" to the logical-ontological question of propositional constituents, and it shows Russell, even at this early stage, insisting on the
intimate connection between the two. Here, however, he fails to enunciate a really precise explanation of the difference between acquaintance
and "knowledge about." This was first provided some years later, in
his essay, "Knowledge by Acquaintance and Knowledge by Description," and in *The Problems of Philosophy*.[2] In these works he contrasts
"knowledge by acquaintance" with "knowledge by description," the
general difference being that the former is "direct" and "immediate,"
whereas the latter is "inferred" and therefore "indirect."

Knowledge by acquaintance is knowledge of things [3] obtained
"without the intermediary of any process of inference or any knowledge of truths." [4] Stated in a more positive way, this means that "I
am *acquainted* with an object when I have a direct cognitive relation to
that object, i.e., when I am directly aware of the object itself." [5] Since
it is a kind of knowledge which does not depend in any way upon inference, it is indubitable, not subject to error. "If I am acquainted with a
thing which exists," Russell maintains, "my acquaintance gives me the
knowledge that it exists." [6] Thus stated, his characterization perhaps
amounts to a truism, but it is, withal, a truism having important epistemological ramifications. The important point to be noticed is that he
does regard acquaintance as a kind of knowing, and, since it provides,
in itself, complete evidence that the object of acquaintance exists, the
knowledge claim it makes is taken to be apodictic, incapable of being
mistaken.

As will become evident, the concept of "acquaintance" is extremely
important in Russell's whole approach to the problem of knowledge of

[1] *L.K.*, pp. 55-56.
[2] This essay first appeared in *Proceedings of the Aristotelian Society*, XI (1910-1911), pp.
108-128. The discussion of this topic in *The Problems of Philosophy* (1912) is essentially the
same as the first half of the earlier version. In the earlier version of the essay there is included
a discussion of knowledge by description as it is related to the theory of descriptions. This
essay has been reprinted in *M.L.*, and page references will be to this source. When referring to
The Problems of Philosophy, I shall employ the pagination of a recent edition (New York and
Oxford, 1959).
[3] Both knowledge by acquaintance and knowledge by description are characterized as
knowledge of *things* and are contrasted with knowledge of *truths*. (Cf. *P.P.*, p. 46.) As we shall
see, knowledge by description *involves* knowledge of truths, but this is only an indication of
its indirectness. It is knowledge *about* things.
[4] *P.P.*, p. 46.
[5] *M.L.*, p. 202.
[6] *P.P.*, p. 45.

the external world. In the first chapter of *P. P.*, where he examines the perennial philosophical question of "appearance and reality," he argues that acquaintance – which he calls there "direct awareness" – is the fundamental kind of empirical knowledge, is, indeed, perhaps the only mode of cognizing external reality to which the term "knowledge" is strictly applicable. Here, emulating Descartes, he engages in a program of systematic doubting, seeking to discover if there is "any knowledge in the world which is so certain that no reasonable man may doubt it." [1] Ultimately, he is sure, our knowledge of the external world must be grounded in those experiences in which we are immediately aware of the world. "In our search for certainty," he maintains, "it is natural to begin with our present experiences, and, in some sense, . . . knowledge is to be derived from them." [2] His quest for the basic elements of our empirical knowledge is, accordingly, conditioned by his assumption that those objects with which a relationship of direct awareness is possible have a privileged status; and he concludes that these objects are always sense-data, never physical objects.

It is not particularly pertinent to explain here precisely how Russell arrives at this conclusion, but, in brief, he rests his argument on what he presumes to be the fact that it is always possible to *doubt* the existence of physical objects, whereas it is not possible to doubt the existence of sense-data.[3] Though, as we shall see, it came to be of first importance for his view of the ontological significance of physical-object symbols, the supposedly dubious nature of our knowledge of physical objects is not, for present purposes, the significant issue. The important point in the context of this examination of knowledge by acquaintance is why acquaintance, or direct awareness, of an object is taken to be an indispensable condition for knowing that that object exists.

The answer to this question is to be located in the fact that Russell, again following Descartes, conceived of empirical knowledge on the paradigm of mathematical or logical knowledge, and, consequently, assumed that, in order to qualify as genuine knowledge, an empirical knowledge claim must be supported by evidence sufficient to establish it as incontrovertibly true. If it is even theoretically possible to doubt that a particular empirical proposition is true, then the claim that the proposition makes is, for him, something less than genuine knowledge, no matter how probable or how relatively well confirmed, in the ordina-

---

[1] *Ibid.*, p. 7.
[2] *Ibid.*
[3] In *P.P.*, however, the objective reality of physical objects is affirmed on the basis of a causal theory of perception.

ry sense, it may be. It is this assumption of what we may call a "certainty theory" of knowing that led him to regard sense-data as the true objects of knowledge in sense experience and to think of knowledge of physical objects as problematic. Sense-data are *presentational* objects, "things immediately known to me just as they are"; [1] to know them we have but to be aware of them, and being aware of them we know them perfectly. For example, "The particular shade of colour that I am seeing may have many things said about it – I may say that it is brown, that it is rather dark, and so on. But such statements, though they make me know truths *about* the colour, do not make me know the colour itself, as opposed to knowledge of truths about it. I know the colour perfectly and completely when I see it, and no further knowledge of itself is even theoretically possible." [2] Being completely "given" in sense experience, sense-data provide both the necessary and sufficient evidence of their existence. Physical objects, on the other hand, are not directly presented in sense experience and are therefore known only indirectly, "by description." This means that physical objects are not, according to the certainty theory of knowing, *known* at all, but only "inferred." Ordinarily, of course, inference is regarded as a perfectly legitimate procedure whereby genuine knowledge may be acquired; since, however, inference of the kind that Russell believes takes place when we pass from sense-data to physical object(s) is at least theoretically capable of being mistaken, it cannot, on his view, be regarded as genuine knowledge.

In connection with this question it will be helpful to consider, for a moment, what Russell means by 'knowledge by description." Of this type of knowledge it can be said, in general, that it "always involves. . . some knowledge of truths as its source and ground." [3] Whatever else this entails, it means, at a minimum, that knowledge by description is not a "direct cognitive relation" with the object known. Rather, we know an object by description when we know that it is *"the* so-and-so, i.e., when we know that there is one object, and no more, having a certain property." [4] This point is well illustrated in a passage from *P. P.* where Russell, using the example of a table, explains how it is that we come to know physical objects:

[1] *Ibid.*, p. 47.
[2] *Ibid.*, pp. 46–47.
[3] *Ibid.*, p. 46.
[4] *M.L.*, p. 207.

"My knowledge of the table is of the kind which we shall call 'knowledge by description.' The table is 'the physical object which causes such-and-such sense-data.' This *describes* the table by means of the sense-data. In order to know anything at all about the table, we must know truths connecting it with things with which we have acquaintance: we must know that 'such-and-such sense-data are caused by a physical object.' There is no state of mind in which we are directly aware of the table; all our knowledge of the table is really knowledge of *truths*, and the actual thing which is the table is not, strictly speaking, known to us at all." [1]

From this passage it is evident, I think, how knowledge by description is fundamentally different from knowledge by acquaintance. In order to know the physical object, even to know that it exists, it must be possible to relate the knowledge we have by acquaintance (of sense-data) with certain "truths" which we bring with us to our experience of the external world. As stated above, this means, for Russell, that knowledge of physical objects is not genuine knowledge; it rests on assumptions and inferences which might conceivably be mistaken.

Perhaps we are now in a position to understand why it is that in the ideal language which Russell envisages, only those words which name objects with which we are acquainted can be regarded as proper names. This conclusion, it seems to me, is reached in the following way: (1) in accordance with the reference theory of meaning, meanings are *objects meant*, entities designated by words functioning as "names"; (2) to understand a word, then, we must know *what* it means, what entity it refers to; (3) since the only genuinely cognizable entities are those with which we are acquainted, it follows that only words designating objects of acquaintance, or words definable in terms of such objects, are intelligible to us. Thus, (4) in an ideal language, all words standing for ultimate constituents (the "logically proper names" of the language) must be words that designate objects with which we are acquainted; otherwise the basic words in the language would be unintelligible.

Clearly, Russell's view that the basic words in a logically perfect language must denote entities with which we are acquainted does not follow solely from the assumptions, primarily the reference theory of meaning, which led him to posit particulars (and relations) as constituents of atomic facts. So conceived, particulars are simply a logical necessity, entities demanded by the linguistic requirement that our basic words have meanings which are definite and unique, not amenable to further analysis. As such, particulars need only be logically "simple" objects. To proceed, as Russell does, to identify particulars

[1] p. 47. Cf. *M.L.*, p. 223.

with those empirical objects which are capable of direct, presentational cognition presupposes a further, far-reaching assumption relating "meaning" to "understanding" and, ultimately, to the theory of acquaintance. This additional assumption played an increasingly large role in Russell's philosophy of language, particularly in his reconstruction of physical-object statements in terms of sense-datum statements. Its legitimacy, as well as that of the reference theory itself, will be examined at the appropriate time.

PROPER NAMES

It is an important consequence of Russell's principle of acquaintance that an ordinary proper name can not be said to function as a logically proper name; for ordinary names, such as "Socrates," do not designate entities with which we are acquainted. According to Russell, "We are not acquainted with Socrates, and therefore cannot name him. When we use the word 'Socrates,' we are really using a description. Our thought may be rendered by some such phrase as 'The Master of Plato,' or 'The philosopher who drank the hemlock,' or 'The person whom logicians assert to be mortal,' but we certainly do not use the name as a name in the proper sense of the word." [1] Russell sometimes writes as though it would be at least theoretically possible to be acquainted with objects designated by ordinary proper names; [2] however, as the preceding discussion of the theory of acquaintance should enable us to see, under no possible circumstances could we be acquainted with such objects: they are simply not the *kind* of entities of which knowledge by acquaintance is possible. As Russell himself points out, the only person who might conceivably be acquainted with a person is that person himself. Speaking of Bismarck, for instance, he says, "if he made a judgement about himself, he himself might be a constituent of the judgement. Here the proper name has the direct use which it always wishes to have, as simply standing for a certain object, and not for a descrip-

[1] *P.L.A.*, p. 201.
[2] Indeed, he says this in some of those very contexts in which he is attempting to make a clear distinction between knowledge by acquaintance and knowledge by description. At one point in *P.P.*, for instance, he implies that it would be possible for him to be acquainted with the Emperor of China, but, as a matter of fact, he is not. (pp. 44–45.) He also says, a few pages later, in a discussion of knowledge by description: "... when we are acquainted with an object which is the so-and-so, we know that the so-and-so exists, but we may know that the so-and-so exists when we are not acquainted with any object which we know to be the so-and-so, and even when we are not acquainted with any object which, in fact, is the so-and-so." (p. 54.) One can only conclude that when he makes statements of this sort he is speaking somewhat loosely and is not thinking of acquaintance in the strict sense discussed above.

tion of the object." [1] In the case of someone else, however, a quite different situation obtains. A person who knows Bismarck is not, strictly speaking, *acquainted* with Bismarck himself. "What this person was acquainted with were certain sense-data which he connected (rightly, we will suppose) with Bismarck's body. His body, as a physical object, and still more his mind, were only known as the body and the mind connected with these sense-data. That is, they were known by description." [2]

It is perhaps not completely clear why, from the circumstance that no one except the person himself could have knowledge by acquaintance of that person, that for no one else could an ordinary proper name function as a logically proper name. In order to understand Russell on this point we must re-invoke the basic assumption underlying the theory of acquaintance, the assumption that all words which are intelligible to us must either directly designate objects of acquaintance or be analyzable in terms of such objects. For Russell, a "person," as ordinarily conceived, has the same kind of "transcendent" or "metaphysical" status that (he believed) physical objects have. Consequently, persons, like physical objects, can be known only by description, as "the so-and-so," the possesssor of certain attributes and qualities with which we may be acquainted. It follows, then, that except for the person himself, no one is acquainted with the entity named by an ordinary proper name. But this means, for Russell, that for everyone except the bearer of the name an ordinary proper name is "unintelligible," since the entity which it (supposedly) names is not, strictly speaking, capable of being known. Thus ordinary proper names cannot function as logically proper names, for in order to qualify as a logically proper name an expression must be, in Russell's narrow sense of the term, "intelligible."

For Russell, also, an ostensible name can only be a genuine (logically proper) name if it cannot be replaced by some description which will serve to convey the meaning we intend to express when we use the name in some proposition. "An atomic proposition," he maintains, "is one which does mention actual particulars, not merely describe them but actually name them . . . ." [3] The only situation in which this can occur is when we use a symbol simply to refer, to point directly to an object, i.e., when we use a symbol *ostensively* to designate an object

[1] *P.P.*, p. 54.
[2] *Ibid.*, p. 55.
[3] *P.L.A.*, p. 200.

with which we are acquainted. The reason for this is that "omitting logical words, the words that we can understand ... must denote things that can, in some case, be pointed out." [1] Whenever a word is used except to "point out," it is functioning not as a name but as a description; and since it is impossible to refer to entities designated by ordinary proper names in this direct way, those words which purport to name them cannot be regarded as genuine proper names.

In addition to the problem just considered, Russell came to feel that there is, regarding ordinary proper names, another, even more fundamental reason why they cannot be considered to be logically proper names. Not only do ordinary proper names really function as descriptions rather than names, the entities they ostensibly name are not such as can legitimately be said to be bearers of proper names. In a sense this is much the same point as the one already made; only objects of acquaintance can be named, and persons are not such objects. In another sense, however, this is a quite different criticism of ordinary proper names than the one just examined. For whereas before Russell had argued that persons are entities which can only be described, not named he is now suggesting that the concept *person* does not designate an entity at all, but is, like the concept *physical object*, analyzable in terms of sets or classes of particulars and is, therefore, what he sometimes calls a "logical fiction."[2] This point is clearly, if somewhat crudely, formulated in *M. P. D.* where he says, "The subject in psychology, and the particle of matter in physics, if they are to be intelligible to us, must both be regarded either as bundles of experienced qualities and relations or as related to such bundles by relations known to experience." [3] The full significance of this passage is not, perhaps, completely clear, but whatever else Russell may be asserting here, he is, at a minimum, suggesting that *person* should not be regarded as an ontologically basic category but, rather, as a kind of "construct" out of data provided through sense experience.

Like the view that ordinary names actually function as descriptions, this view also, I believe, ultimately rests on the assumption that only objects of acquaintance can be said to be known, though in this case the way in which the assumption is involved is less direct and therefore less immediately evident. It would seem, however, that Russell's attempt to interpret persons as "bundles of experienced qualities

[1] *M.P.D.*, p. 169.
[2] Cf. *P.L.A.*, p. 191.
[3] p. 170.

and relations" results, ultimately, from his conviction that persons, as ordinarily conceived, are, according to the theory of acquaintance, strictly unknowable. Though he was, for a time, either imperfectly aware of the seriousness of the implications of the theory of acquaintance for knowledge of persons, or thought he could circumvent them with his notion of "knowledge by description," he did finally come to believe that the difficulties occasioned by this theory were extreme and could not be avoided in any such way. Consequently, he found it desirable to reconstruct the concept *person* in such a way that it be taken to designate sets or classes of sense-given particulars and relations, which, since they can be objects of acquaintance, can be known. Russell concludes: "we shall say that a person is a certain series of experiences. We shall not deny that there may be a metaphysical ego. We shall merely say that it is a question that does not concern us in any way, because it is a matter about which we know nothing and can know nothing, and therefore it obviously cannot be a thing that comes into science in any way. What we know is this string of experiences that makes up a person, and that is put together by means of certain empirically given relations ...." [1] This conclusion represents a clear and significant triumph, in Russell's thought, for the theory of acquaintance; for it shows him willing to reconstruct a basic ontological category of ordinary language in order to satisfy the requirement that the fundamental entities in our ontology be knowable in the only way this theory deems authentic.

Since ordinary proper names do not satisfy the requirements for logically proper names, it is, Russell points out, "very difficult to get any instance of a name at all in the proper strict sense of the word." [2] What is required, we have noted, is some word or words which directly refer to objects without describing them in any way. According to him, the only words which function in this way are the demonstratives "this" and "that," for they, and only they, can be used to refer to an object in such a direct manner that it would be impossible to replace them with a description. As he says, "The only words one does use as names in the logical sense are words like 'this' and 'that.' One can use 'this' as a name to stand for a particular with which one is acquainted at the moment. We say 'This is white.' If you agree that 'This is white,' meaning the 'this' that you see, you are using 'this' as a proper name. But if you try to apprehend the proposition that I am expressing when

---

[1] *Ibid.*, p. 277.
[2] *Ibid.*, p. 201.

I say 'This is white,' you cannot do it. If you mean this piece of chalk as a physical object, then you are not using a proper name. It is only when you use 'this' quite strictly, to stand for an actual object of sense, that it is really a proper name." [1] In this passage we again encounter the doctrine that logically proper names can be applied only to objects of acquaintance; consequently physical objects cannot be named. In addition, two thoughts are here given expression for the first time which show the truly radical character of Russell's views concerning logically proper names: (1) a logically proper name, insofar as it is functioning *as* a name, cannot designate the same object for two different people; and (2) a logically proper name can designate only those entities with which we are acquainted *at the moment*. It is, of course, primarily for these two reasons that Russell regards demonstratives as the only genuine names, for they alone, he believes, have the capacity to denote objects in the "ambiguous" way required of a symbol which must constantly designate different objects – to different people at one and the same time, and to the same person at different times. Speaking of the word "this" as it functions in the language, he says, "it has a very odd property for a proper name, namely that it seldom means the same thing two moments running and does not mean the same thing to the speaker and to the hearer. It is an *ambiguous* proper name, but it is really a proper name all the same, and it is almost the only thing I can think of that is used properly and logically in the sense that I was talking of a proper name." [2]

Though this aspect of Russell's conception of proper names may seem so removed from the ordinary conception as to appear almost fantastic, it is, I think, an inevitable consequence of a consistent adherence to his theory of acquaintance in the quest for logically proper names. Indeed, if we grant his premises – that we can only name those objects with which we are acquainted, and that the only objects with which we are acquainted are sense-data – then we have, in effect, already accepted this conclusion. For, strictly speaking, we know by acquaintance only those sense-data of which we are directly aware at a given moment; and these sense-data are at least numerically different from any sense-data we ourselves may have at some other time or which any other person may be aware of, either at the same time or at any other time. It follows, then, that when we use the word "this" to designate some object of acquaintance, what it denotes will be different

---

[1] *Ibid.*
[2] *Ibid.*

from moment to moment and will never be any object with which any-
one else is acquainted. And since, on the reference theory of meaning,
the meaning of a word is the object to which it refers, this entails, for
Russell, that the *meaning* of "this" changes every time it is used to
designate a different object; consequently, its meaning is constantly
changing.

With the discovery of demonstratives as the only logically proper
names, Russell's search for the words in the basic propositions of an
ideal language which are capable of standing for particulars is completed. In the ideal language which he envisages, all words which function as names can be used only in the actual presence of the object being
named, and this has the consequence that "as regards its vocabulary,
[a logically perfect language] would be largely private to one speaker." [1]
The "simple objects" for which there is to be "one word and no more"
are, then sense-data, and the words which stand for them must be, in
a properly reconstructed language, the demonstratives "this" and
"that." Only when we have accomplished this reconstruction – or at
least have shown how it may be accomplished – can we feel secure in
our knowledge that grammar will not mislead us concerning the true
forms of propositions.

Typically, Russell does not even attempt to carry out an actual
reconstruction of ordinary language. At most, he suggests how various
particular types of propositions could be re-cast so as to improve their
forms. One major reason for this somewhat casual approach to the actual reconstruction of ordinary language may have been simply that
he did not see the necessity of working out the details of this program.
His main interest, it seems, was in calling attention to the *theoretical
need* for such a reconstruction. He seems to have been little interested
in a project of this type conceived as a philosophical end in itself.
Rather, he was concerned to show that there are pressing reasons why
the theoretical goal of reconstructionism is philosophically requisite.
Once having shown this, he apparently felt that the important philosophical task had been accomplished.

As I have tried to make clear, by far the most important specific task
for the philosopher, in connection with the reconstruction of ordinary
language, is, Russell believed, the discovery of those linguistic expressions which have a genuinely referential function. If, in the preceding

---

[1] *Ibid.*, p. 198. Russell does not explain why he qualifies his statement as he does, using the
words "very largely." Perhaps he has in mind that words for relations would not be "private"
(i.e., their "meanings" would not be private).

discussion of the ideal language as he envisaged it, I have been concerned almost exclusively with the question of words standing for particulars, and have said little or nothing about the over-all structure of atomic propositions or the relationships which, in an ideal language, would be seen to hold between them, this largely because he himself had little to say about such matters. Russell's main concern was to determine which words ostensibly referring to particulars are genuinely referential and which are merely incomplete symbols and are therefore dispensable. His efforts, therefore, were dedicated to the discovery of those symbols which can *not* be eliminated from language because they denote entities so ontologically basic that their removal would leave us without any foundation on which to build the enormous and complex edifice which is ordinary language.

THE "MINIMUM VOCABULARY"

Russell's procedure here may, I think, be compared with the procedure he followed in *P. M.* in seeking the minimal logical apparatus from which he believed the whole of mathematics could, ultimately, be derived. Regarding this point, Professor Urmson has suggested that not only in the general method of analysis it recommended, but in other, more specific, respects, the *P. M.* logic may have influenced Russell's logical atomist position. The comparison Urmson makes between the *P. M.* logic and Russell's logical atomism seems, on the whole, a bit overdrawn; nevertheless there is much to be said for it. Particularly sound, it seems to me, is the suggestion that Russell's work in mathematical logic may have led him to try to use a method and techniques similar to those he had employed there to reduce mathematics to a few logical premises, to clarify ordinary language and "reduce" it to its fundamental propositions and, beyond that, to the basic constituents of these propositions. Urmson summarizes this point as follows: "as the techniques of logic could define and thus make theoretically superfluous the more complex and abstruse concepts of mathematics, so, by the application of the same techniques the less concrete items of the furniture of heaven and earth ... could be defined and theoretically eliminated."[1]

Standing in support of this interpretation are several statements of Russell's in *P. L. A.*, one of which I have chosen for extended quotation. In the concluding lecture, after explaining that one of his purposes

---

[1] J. O. Urmson, *Philosophical Analysis* (Oxford, 1956), p. 6.

throughout the preceding lectures has been "the justification of analysis," he continues,

Another purpose that runs through all that I have been saying is the purpose embodied in the maxim called Occam's Razor. That maxim comes in, in practice, in this way: taken some science, say physics. You have there a given body of doctrine, a set of propositions expressed in symbols – I am including words among symbols – and you think that you have reason to believe that on the whole those propositions, rightly interpreted, are fairly true, but you do not know what is the actual meaning of the symbols that you are using .... you go through, if you are analysing a science like physics, these propositions with a view to finding out what is the smallest empirical apparatus – or the smallest apparatus, not necessarily wholly empirical – out of which you can build up these propositions. What is the smallest number of simple undefined things at the start, and the smallest number of undemonstrated premisses, out of which you can define the things that need to be defined and prove the things that need to be proved? That problem, in any case that you like to take, is by no means a simple one, but on the contrary an extremely difficult one. It is one which requires a very great amount of logical technique; and the sort of thing that I have been talking about in these lectures is the preliminaries and first steps in that logical technique.[1]

In this passage Russell delineates his method in quite general terms and does not spell out what the "logical technique" to which he refers consists in.[2] A more specific characterization of the method he advocated – and employed – not only in *P. L. A.* but consistently throughout the logical atomist period (as well as later) is provided in *M. P. D.* where, attempting to explicate his assertion that "Names ... can only be given to something experienced, whether in sense or in thought,"[3] he says,

Perhaps the matter may be made clearer by introducing what I have called 'minimum vocabularies.' These are defined as follows: given any body of sentences which we can understand, what is the smallest number of words in terms of which all the other words of the sentences in question can be defined? In general, there is not a unique answer to this question, but the different possible answers will, as a rule, contain some words common to them all. These words represent the hard core of experience by which our sentences are attached to the non-linguistic world .... We may perhaps define the 'stuff' of the world as what is designated by words which, when correctly used, occur as subjects of predicates or terms of relations.[4]

---

[1] pp. 270–271.

[2] He does, however, proceed immediately to describe what is clearly one important instance of it, the logical construction of physical objects, or, as he refers to it here, the construction of "logical fictions" which are to replace physical objects qua metaphysical entities.

[3] p. 169.

[4] p. 170; Cf. *P.B.R.*, pp. 14ff, 687ff. It should be noted, in passing, that in *M.P.D.* Russell no longer holds the view that "particulars" constitute the basic furniture of the world, stating in a sentence I have omitted, that "I do not believe that ... there are any [words] having the kind of uniqueness supposed to belong to [words for] particulars." (p. 170). For my purposes, however, this fact is irrelevant, since the characterization of his method just cited applied to the method he employed in his logical atomist period no less than to the later stages of his philosophy. The method, indeed, is precisely the same; only his conclusions are different.

Later, in this same work, ostensibly replying to criticisms of mathematical logic offered by G. J. Warnock, Russell makes these pertinent remarks:

The relation of logic to ontology is ... very complex. We can in some degree separate linguistic aspects of this problem from those that have a bearing on ontology. The linguistic problems are capable, at least in theory, of a precise solution, but the ontological problems remain much more obscure. The purely linguistic problems, however, have an ontological background, though a somewhat vague one. Sentences are composed of words, and, if they are to able be to assert facts, some, at least, of the words must have that kind of relation to something else that is called 'meaning.' ... This degree of ontological commitment is involved in all ordinary speech. But the relation of words to objects other than words varies according to the kind of word concerned, and this gives rise to a logical form of the doctrine of parts of speech. If a sentence is to have significance, unless it is a sentence of pure logic, some of its words must point to something, but others need not .... A large part of the bearing of mathematical logic upon ontology consists in diminishing the number of objects required in order to make sense of statements which we feel to be intelligible. The only reason for this process of whittling away is to avoid rash and unwarranted assumptions. If our ordinary empirical statements are to be significant, they must ... point to something outside words. The purely technical question thus arises: what is the smallest vocabulary which will enable us to assert what we believe to be fact?" [1]

I have quoted Russell at length here because it seems to me that nowhere else does he characterize his general philosophical method so explicitly, particularly those aspects of his philosophy which have bearing on his philosophy of language. We may, I think, regard his whole reconstructionist program as an effort to secure a "minimum vocabulary" which would provide the basic terms for the logically perfect language he envisages as the ultimate goal of reconstructionism. This vocabulary, as the passages just cited have indicated, would be, in effect, the *indispensable* types of symbols remaining after the superfluous words have been extirpated or, rather, "reduced" to, defined in terms of, words which function referentially. The important fact to keep in mind is that this quest for a minimum vocabulary had, for Russell, genuine ontological significance. He was convinced that if we can discover it, the symbols it includes will be those which stand for objects which we should regard as the basic "stuff" of the world. When we have analyzed our language and have eliminated from it such vocabulary as appears to be mere excess baggage, the residue will be those symbols which must be taken as having ontological significance, as denoting some basic reality. These will be the ultimate "premisses" from which the remainder of ordinary language is derived; therefore those parts of ordinary language

[1] pp. 235–236.

which are built upon them, the "incomplete symbols," can be regarded as having only such ontological significance as the basic words possess, and propositions containing such symbols will be capable of interpretation in terms of these more basic symbols.

The analysis of propositions must, of course, proceed on the basis of certain assumptions which provide criteria for determining what entities are to be regarded as ontologically basic. Defined only as "terms of relations in atomic facts," particulars need have no special character in order to qualify as particulars, except that of being "simple," and this, in itself, tells us very little, since, depending upon the criteria of simplicity that one employs, any number of things might qualify as simple. Our previous examination of the theory of acquaintance, however, has indicated – and the passages just cited attest – that, for Russell, the fundamental consideration governing any investigation of this type should be the cognitive status of the entity in question. This, we have seen, reduces to the question of the entity's epistemic accessibility, and this, in turn, was seen to be equivalent to the question of whether it could be an object of acquaintance. Those alleged entities which are inherently incapable of being cognized in the direct way required in order to qualify as objects of acquaintance must be considered suspect, and every effort must be made to interpret them in terms of entities which are objects of acquaintance. It may be difficult, perhaps it is impossible, to define all our words in terms of words designating objects known by acquaintance, but it is the goal for which we should set our sights. Insofar as this is not accomplished, insofar as we fail to show, in principle at least, how we can define constituent-words in terms of words which "represent the hard core of experience by which our sentences are attached to the world," we fail to provide for them, and for the propositions in which they occur, a genuine meaning.

SUMMARY AND CONCLUSION

It seems, then, that in the notion of a "minimum vocabulary," a point has been reached in our investigation at which the various doctrines associated with the concept of "logical form" – reconstructionism, the ideal language ,and the principle of acquaintance – become so assimilated to one another as to be virtually inseparable. Moreover, it can now be seen more clearly that the search for logical form has important ontological significance, for the minimum vocabulary is taken to be that set of symbols which denote entities that are ontologically basic. The preceding discussion of "logical form" may, then, be summarized in the following way: in the wide sense, logical form is the structure of a proposition clarified with respect to both syntax and vocabulary. It is clarified when its structure is exhibited as isomorphic with the basic structure of the fact it asserts. Essential for such clarification is the elimination of incomplete symbols and the exhibition of the true constituents of the propositions. These constituents – those remaining in a properly reconstructed proposition – denote ontologically basic entities and are all names of objects known by acquaintance.

Thus far I have attempted to present a rather synoptic picture of Russell's philosophy of language and the assumptions on which it rests, based, for the most part, on his own statements. I have tried to show that, fundamentally, this method aims at the reconstruction of propositions of ordinary language which, due to the presence of "incomplete symbols," misrepresent the logical forms of the facts they assert. Though I have given a cursory account of what reconstruction is and have illustrated the use of this method in the analysis of three kinds of propositions, a precise rendering of what it involves remains to be provided. In the following chapter, therefore, I shall take a closer and more detailed look at reconstructionism. I shall proceed by examining Russell's use of this method in the actual analysis of several kinds of proposition. As before, I shall consider the reconstruction of propositions containing descriptive phrases, those containing class-symbols, and those containing symbols for physical objects.

CHAPTER II

THE USES OF RECONSTRUCTIONISM

In the previous chapter I described reconstructionism, quite generally, as a method of analysis whereby propositions in ordinary language are reformulated so as to rid them of their misleading grammatical forms and exhibit the true constituents of facts they may assert. So characterized, reconstructionism may be said to represent the common denominator of a number of somewhat diverse analytic techniques employed by Russell at various times, collected under a single rubric. Professor Weitz has suggested – correctly, I believe – that there is a basic similarity between the analytic techniques Russell calls, variously, (1) the analysis of denoting phrases, (2) the analysis of incomplete symbols, (3) constructionism, and (4) the principle which dispenses with abstractionism.[1] All of these, it seems to me, aim at accomplishing the purpose I have indicated as the overall aim of reconstructionism, taken as a general method. As I am using the term, then, "reconstructionism" signifies not so much a single method as a "family" of analytic methods that have an essentially common function.

A survey of Russell's writings will disclose a number of analyses of various kinds which, though differing in certain respects, are yet sufficiently similar to warrant classification as "reconstructions" of one type or another. These include, besides the three noted in the previous chapter, his analyses of "number," "instant," and "point," and several others could perhaps be cited. In all of these cases, regardless of differences of approach or formulation they may present, the analytic procedure involves a recasting of the proposition containing an expression of a certain type so that, in the resultant proposition, the expression will have disappeared, and with it the temptation to assume the existence of some entity corresponding to the expression.

---

[1] See *P.B.R.*, p. 92. Weitz adds to this list "the logical-analytic method." I would agree that in some instances of Russell's use of this method he is engaged in the same kind of analysis that characterizes the other four techniques, but not, I think, in all of them.

It must not be inferred from this, however, that the different instances of reconstructionism were the result of a carefully formulated "program" of analysis. Such was not the case. Rather, each analysis was provided as the problem which it was designed to meet waxed importunate and demanded resolution. Insofar as the analyses in question are similar, they reflect a somewhat desultory application of the general precept with which Russell operated throughout most of his philosophical writings, that the goal of philosophical analysis is to secure a "minimum vocabulary." Adherence to this principle, which he frequently refers to as his version of Occam's Razor,[1] seems to have provided the motivation for undertaking a particular analysis once the occasion for it arose; but it did not issue in a systematic attempt to reconstruct language.

Although his analysis of "number" as "a class of similar classes" in *P. of M.*[2] may be regarded as the first instance of his use of reconstructionism, it was the theory of descriptions that suggested to Russell the value reconstructionism might have as a general analytic method. As we saw in the previous chapter, it was his analysis of descriptive phrases which led him to realize that analysis is necessary to determine the true logical status of expressions presumed to function referentially. This theory, then, is the most feasible starting point for an investigation of the nature and function of reconstructionism. In the following pages I shall examine it in sufficient detail to show (a) the nature of the problem that led to its formulation; (b) how it represents an attempt to meet this problem through reconstructing language; and (c) precisely what is involved in exhibiting descriptions as "incomplete symbols."

THE THEORY OF DESCRIPTIONS [3]

In *P. of M.* Russell's analysis of descriptions forms a part of his examination of "denoting concepts." A denoting concept he describes as one formed by annexing to a class-concept one of the following six words : *all, every, any, a, some* ,or *the*. In order to describe something we must, he maintains, use one of these concepts to designate a term of some kind. (A term, it will be recalled, he defined as "whatever may be an object of thought, or may occur in any true or false proposition, or

---

[1] Cf. *O.K.E.W.*, pp. 86, 116; *P.L.A.*, p. 221; *P.B.R.*, pp. 13, 63, 71, 103.

[2] Cf. pp. 116f.

[3] The discussion in this section will be based on Russell's views as set forth in the following works: *P. of M.*, (pp. 53–65, 502); "On Denoting," (*L. K.*, pp. 41–56); *P. M.*, (pp. 66–71); *P.L.A.* (*L.K.*, pp. 232f., 241–254); *I.M.P.*, (pp. 167–180).

may be regarded as one.") All terms are entities of some kind, whether they be physical objects, relations, properties, fictional beings, or whatever. Thus, he concludes, the role of a description in a sentence is always to stand for some term, to designate some kind of entity.

With this as background we can better understand the nature of the problem that led him to formulate his theory of descriptions. In *P. of M.* his view of the logical function of denoting concepts (or, as I shall say alternatively, denoting phrases or descriptive phrases) is relatively simple and uncomplicated. A concept preceded by one of the six words just mentioned denotes some term, regardless of what the concept may be. Here, clearly, Russell is thinking of denoting concepts on the analogy of proper names. Indeed, in one of the appendices to this work he criticizes Frege's claim that names have both a "meaning" and an "indication" (a "sense" and a "reference") [1] on the grounds that "only such proper names as are derived from concepts by means of *the* can be said to have meaning." [2] The implication of this statement is, of course, that those expressions formed by prefixing "the" to some class concept (i.e., definite descriptions) have a logical function similar to that of ordinary proper names, the only difference being that they have a meaning (or, more precisely, a connotation) whereas ordinary proper names do not. Both kinds of expression, however, are thought to refer directly to some entity which is the referent of the expression.

Several considerations, however, caused Russell to revise this view of denoting phrases, and in "On Denoting" he attacks Meinong and Frege for holding views similar to it. The general defect of an interpretation of descriptions as names, he now feels, is that it cannot do justice to those cases in which the uniqueness condition is not satisfied, to those cases, that is, in which there is either nothing at all or not precisely *one* entity answering the description. Treating descriptions as names seems plausible enough when we are dealing only with sentences in which the entity described actually exists. It seems quite natural to interpret a statement such as "The thirty-sixth president of the United States is a Democrat" as a statement *about* the person who is the thirty-sixth president, Lyndon B. Johnson. (In cases where the entity described *no longer* exists, e.g., "The master of Plato was forced to drink hem-

[1] The distinction in question is that between what Frege calls "Sinn" and "Bedeutung." This distinction is found in G. Frege, "Über Sinn und Bedeutung," *Zeitschrift für Philosophie und Philosophische Kritik*, C (1892), 25–50. This essay has been reprinted, in English translation, in H. Feigl and W. Sellars (eds.) *Readings in Philosophical Analysis*, (New York, 1949), pp. 85–109.

[2] p. 502.

lock," the situation is not in any relevant sense different.) There are countless instances, however, in which the object described does not now exist and has never existed (e.g., "the golden mountain") and instances in which the object described could not conceivably exist, because its concept involves a self-contradiction (e.g., "the round square"). Moreover, there are cases in which the description attempts to designate as unique an individual that may exist but is not unique (e.g., "the inhabitant of London"). If descriptions are names it would appear that in cases in which the uniqueness condition is not satisfied the sentence in which the description occurs would be about nothing at all and would therefore be meaningless. In many cases, however, such sentences are not only meaningful but true. Faced with the problem of accounting for their meaningfulness we can, Russell suggests, do one of two things: (1) we can continue to assume that descriptive phrases function referentially and try to formulate a conception of their denotata that will make it possible to say that even in those instances in which the uniqueness condition is unfulfilled (or would ordinarily be said to be unfulfilled) there is still a denotatum of some type; or (2) we can try to find some interpretation of these phrases that dispenses with this assumption, so that the problem of the denotata of vacuous descriptions does not arise. Meinong and Frege, in different ways, take the first alternative; Russell, the second.

Meinong's solution to the problem is the heroic one. It amounts to denying that there are, in fact, vacuous descriptive phrases. For him all descriptions, including those that describe non-existent and self-contradictory entities, designate some object. He distinguishes three general classes of entities: (1) impossible objects, (2) possible but non-actual objects, and (3) actual objects. Only objects included under (3) exist, but those objects in (1) and (2) also have some kind of being and can be denotata of descriptive phrases. Thus existence is, for him, as it was for Russell in *P. of M.*, only one of several modes of being; consequently he finds it possible to assign a referential function to all descriptive phrases. Even if they do not have the fullblown reality of existing things, all objects described have a kind of being that permits them to possess properties and function as terms of relations.

Meinong's theory admits into the world all sorts of "objects" posessing various types and degrees of reality. Frege's solution is similar in that it too postulates referents for descriptive phrases in cases where we would ordinarily say there are none. His postulata, however, are, as he realizes, simply conventions which are proposed in order to remedy a formal defect he finds in natural languages, viz., that in some cases an expression of the form " the so-and-so" designates an object whereas in other cases it does not.[1] In those cases where there is no object corresponding to the description he suggests that special conventions be adopted whereby the description be *assigned* a conventional descriptum of some kind. For example, expressions which stand for no existing entity (e.g., "the present king of France") can be said to designate the null-class, definite descriptions that attempt to designate uniquely one of several members of a class (e.g., "the inhabitant of London") can be said to designate the class itself, and so on.

Let us consider now Russell's criticisms of these views, beginning with his criticism of Meinong. One difficulty of Meinong's interpretation of descriptive phrases, he suggests, is that in postulating objects corresponding to descriptions that do not designate any *existing* thing, we "are apt to infringe the law of contradiction."[2] Russell's point here is that if we assume the existence of some "object" such as the golden mountain or the round square we seem to contradict ourselves if we assert, as we truthfully may, that the entity in question does not exist. "For if there were such an object, it would exist; we cannot first assume that there is a certain object, and then proceed to deny that there is such an object."[3] Strictly speaking, Meinong's theory does not, it is true, violate the law of contradiction. But it avoids doing so only by postulating several modes of being, participation in which does not entail that an object *exist*. If the kind of being peculiar to, say, fictional entities is ascribed to it, it is possible to assert, consistently, both that this object *is* in some sense and that it does not exist.

In "On Denoting" Russell rejects Meinong's postulation of various kinds of "unreal" objects almost without explanation, saying only that this course "is to be avoided as much as possible." In *I.M.P.*, however, he articulates those convictions relative to this point which it seems plausible to assume were also operative in the earlier work:

The question of 'unreality,' which confronts us at this point, is a very important one. Misled by grammar, the great majority of those logicians who have dealt with this question have dealt with it on mistaken lines. They have regarded grammatical form as a surer guide in analysis than, in fact, it is. And they have not known what differences in grammatical form are important. . . . it is argued, *e.g.* by Meinong, that we can speak about 'the golden mountain,' 'the round square,' and so on; we can make true propositions of which these are the subjects; hence they must have some kind of logical being, since otherwise the propositions

---

[1] Cf. Feigl and Sellars, p. 95.

[2] *L.K.*, p. 45.

[3] *P.M.*, p. 66.

in which they occur would be meaningless. In such theories, it seems to me, there is a failure of that feeling for reality which ought to be preserved even in the most abstract studies. Logic, I should maintain, must no more admit a unicorn than zoology can; for logic is concerned with the real world just as truly as zoology, though with its more abstract and general features.[1]

Two points are given expression in this passage that serve to illumine Russell's criticism of Meinong's procedure. His postulation of entities to serve as referents of descriptions that do not satisfy the uniqueness condition is, Russell suggests, unsatisfactory because (1) it is gratuitous and (2) it offends our "feeling for reality."

(1) It is gratuitous because it has its genesis in his assumption that the grammatical forms of propositions are a reliable index of their logical forms. Russell's meaning here, I believe, is that Meinong takes the grammatical similarity between propositions containing names and those containing descriptive phrases as a sign of their logical similarity and therefore assumes that because descriptive phrases may function as *grammatical* subjects of propositions, they are, like proper names, the *logical* subjects of these propositions. Consequently, he concludes that these propositions are about objects designated by the descriptions. It follows, then, that if the propositions are meaningful there must be some entity corresponding to each description. Here, however, Meinong is "misled by grammar." for, Russell argues, the grammatical forms of propositions containing descriptive phrases are radically different from their logical forms and do not presuppose, for their meaningfulness, that there be some entity corresponding to each description. (This will be explained presently.)

(2) In deprecating Meinong's theory as repugnant to our "feeling for reality," Russell is, I think, suggesting that in our approach to questions of logical analysis, we must not simply ignore the logical and ontological framework of ordinary language. We have a responsibility to this framework and our analyses must not do violence to it. Within it, it is inconsistent to attribute a kind of being to non-existent entities, and we cannot postulate such entities simply in order to make sense of our presuppositions as to how language functions. A theory that incorporates postulation of this type is to be held suspect even if it is adequate on other grounds.

Of Frege's method Russell says that it is "plainly artificial and does not give an exact analysis of the matter." [2] Russell perhaps misses the point of Frege's proposal to provide a purely conventional referent in

---

[1] *Introduction to Mathematical Philosophy* (London, 1919), pp. 168–169.
[2] *L.K.*, p. 47.

those cases in which the uniqueness condition is not satisfied. Frege's aim in doing so is to correct what he takes to be a formal defect in ordinary language, and his proposal would make it possible to interpret all descriptive phrases as names and would therefore be an important step in the construction of a language system having more logical elegance than do ordinary languages. Russell, however, does not regard this as a genuine solution to the problem since it does not provide an analysis of the way descriptions actually function in language. It *assumes* that they function in a certain way and then employs stipulation to take care of difficult cases.

Russell's own solution proceeds from his denial that descriptions function logically as names. Therefore, regardless of whether there is or is not some entity corresponding to a particular descriptive phrase, that phrase does not *name* the entity. His analysis of descriptions has two steps. First he presents arguments based on an examination of the different ways names and descriptions actually function in language to show the logical differences between them. Then he shows how description-propositions [1] can be reconstructed so that their true logical form is made evident.

The most important arguments in support of the view that descriptions and names have different logical functions are the following:

(1) There is, first, the circumstance that if a description, e.g., "the author of *Waverley*," functioned as a name, it could be replaced by some name, either "Scott" or some other. If it were replaced by "Scott" the proposition "Scott is the author of *Waverley*" would become the trivial identity "Scott is Scott." If replaced by any other name, *c*, the resulting proposition "Scott is *c*" would be false. The original proposition, however, was neither trivial nor false, but genuinely informative.[2]

(2) If "the author of *Waverley*" were a name, it would apply to Scott merely by virtue of the fact that he was *called* "the author of *Waverley*." As the phrase is being used in the proposition "Scott is the author of *Waverley*" however, Scott is not designated "the author of *Waverley*" because he is called that, but because of something he did. This point is easily seen if we contrast this proposition with one in which we assert a relationship between two names, e.g., "Scott was Sir Walter."[3]

(3) A name is a simple symbol whereas a description, since it contains

---

[1] I shall frequently employ this expression and the expressions "description-sentence" and "description-statement" as abbreviated forms of "propositions (sentences, statements) containing descriptive phrases." All of these are to be taken as having the same meaning.

[2] Cf. *P.M.*, p. 67; *P.L.A.*, p. 245; *I.M.P.*, p. 174.

[3] Cf. *P.M.*, p. 67; *P.L.A.*, pp. 244f; *I.M.P.*, p. 174.

parts that are themselves symbols, is complex. It follows from this that the meaning of a description is *determinate*, for if the meanings of its parts are given, *its* meaning is given. The meaning of a name, however, is indeterminate, because it means only what it is *arbitrarily* designated to name.[1]

If descriptions do not function as names, there is no special problem connected with those descriptions that do not satisfy the uniqueness condition. Neither descriptions that do nor descriptions that do not satisfy the uniqueness condition designate entities; therefore the meaningfulness of a proposition is not contingent on this condition being satisfied. The question may be raised, however: if descriptions are not names, what are the propositions in which they occur *about*? In the case of a proposition in which the descriptive phrase appears as the grammatical subject in a subject-predicate sentence, to what, if not the denotatum of the description, is the predicate being ascribed?

The difficulty with this question, Russell suggests, is that it presupposes more than is warranted about the logical forms of propositions containing descriptive phrases. Specifically, it presupposes that because a description-sentence may take the subject-predicate form it is therefore an assertion about some entity designated by the subject term. This, however, is not the case, and once shorn of their misleading grammatical dress these sentences exhibit a form quite different from that of true subject-predicate sentences. For properly clarified they are seen to be not singular propositions at all, but general existential propositions concerning a property or properties possessed by some (unique) individual.

For Russell, clarification of these propositions is effected by translating them into that set of statements that imply, and are implied by, the original proposition. In order to see what this involves we may consider the familiar example, "The author of *Waverley* was Scotch." There are, Russell suggests, three statements which this sentence implies and which, taken together, imply it:

(1) someone wrote *Waverley*;
(2) only one person wrote *Waverley*;
(3) whoever wrote *Waverley* was Scotch.

(1) and (2) together mean that the (unique) person who wrote *Waverley* exists, i.e.,

$$(\exists c) \; [Wc . (x) \; (Wx \equiv x = c)].$$

[1] Cf. *P.L.A.*, p. 244; *I.M.P.*, p. 174.

(3) simply adds that this person was Scotch. The symbolic expression of the entire sentence is, then,

$$(\exists c) \, [Wc.(x) \, (Wx \equiv x = c).Sc].$$

Symbolized in this way, it is evident how different is its form from a sentence in which a name occurs in the place of the descriptive phrase. The form of "Scott was Scotch" for instance (assuming "Scott" as a genuine name) is shown in the simple expression, $S_{(s)}$.

Because "Scott" is a proper name [1] it must be represented as an element in the symbolic expression of any sentence in which it occurs. In the reconstructed version of the sentence containing the phrase "the author of *Waverley*," however, no symbol for the phrase, as such, appears. This indicates that it is not a constituent of the sentence; consequently it can only be defined contextually ("in use") by translating the whole sentence in which it occurs. If descriptions were genuine constituents of sentences it would not be necessary to give them a contextual definition in order to show what they "mean." They would have meaning "in isolation" and would appear as indissoluble elements in any re-statement of any proposition in which they occur. For if, as Russell believed, his reconstruction of description-propositions succeeds in clarifying their logical form, it would follow, on his assumption of an isomorphism between fact and (clarified) proposition, that those expressions that are genuine constituents will remain in the reconstructed proposition. They are, for him, the linguistic correlates of constituents of facts and without them it would be impossible to say everything asserted by the original proposition. Since descriptions can be eliminated altogether they are shown to be "incomplete symbols." This, as we saw earlier, means that they do not have a referential function. According to Russell, "Whenever the grammatical subject of a proposition can be supposed not to exist without rendering the proposition meaningless, it is plain that the grammatical subject is not a proper name, i.e., not a name directly representing some object." [2] Since descriptions do not function referentially, description-propositions are not "about" their (supposed) referents; consequently, they do not presuppose for their meaningfulness that such objects exist.

We see, then, that the theory of descriptions has not only logical but ontological significance. In exhibiting descriptions as incomplete symbols, Russell has shown that we need not assume that they designate

---

[1] Or at least may be taken to be a name here.
[2] *P.M.*, p. 66.

objects which must be included in our ontological inventory of the world. This is not to say, of course, that there are no objects corresponding to an enormous number of descriptive phrases. The value of the theory of descriptions, insofar as it has bearing on questions of ontology, is that it vitiates the claim that we *must* include "objects denoted" in our ontological inventory in order to account for the meaningfulness of description-sentences. Russell's theory makes it evident that this is an unnecessary assumption and that it results from confusing logical with grammatical form.

So far I have shown that Russell's theory of descriptions is, in some sense, an analysis of description-sentences that aims at explicating their true meanings and their true logical forms. It is not clear, however, from what has been said so far, in precisely *what sense* Russell's theory provides an analysis of the forms of description-sentences. Russell's own statements on this point are somewhat vague. In *I.M.P.*, for example,[1] discussing the analysis of "The author of *Waverley* was Scotch" into the three sentences listed above he says, ". . . the three together may be taken as defining what is meant by the proposition 'the author of *Waverley* was Scotch.'" It is the phrase "may be taken as" that is disturbing here.[2] It is not clear whether Russell is making a *proposal* (or a *stipulation*) that, for certain purposes, the original sentence is *to be interpreted as* meaning what the three sentences, taken together, mean; or whether he is saying that the three sentences taken conjointly assert, in a less misleading way, the meaning the original proposition has in ordinary language. Let us consider these two possibilities.

According to Carnap the theory of descriptions is "[a proposal] for an interpretation and, consequently, for deductive rules, concerning descriptions in symbolic systems."[3] It is not, he maintains, intended as an analysis of the meaning of phrases of the form 'the so-and-so' in English. Therefore, in order to determine its adequacy we must not ask whether it is the "correct" analysis; rather, we should inquire into its "comparative convenience" as a method for translating description-sentences. This can be accomplished by comparing it with other methods, e.g., that of Frege. Assuming this interpretation the relationship between Russell's theory of descriptions and ordinary language would

---

[1] p. 177.

[2] G. E. Moore calls attention to the vagueness of this phrase and concludes that Russell means that the three sentences *do* define what is meant by the original statement. (See his essay, "Russell's 'Theory of Descriptions'," in *P.B.R.*, pp. 175–225. See especially pp. 182f.) Russell's reply to Moore (*P.B.R.*, p. 691) does little to clarify this point.

[3] Rudolf Carnap, *Meaning and Necessity* (Chicago, 1956), p. 33.

be extremely tenuous. It would be, in effect, a stipulation that description-sentences are to be translated in a certain way. As such it would be on a par with Frege's proposal to assign a conventional descriptum to descriptions that do not satisfy the uniqueness condition. Neither theory would provide an analysis of ordinary language as such; both would simply use ordinary language as a point of departure in the construction of a language system which is intended to be technically superior, in certain respects, to ordinary language.[1]

A quite contrary interpretation is suggested by M. Black.[2] Black regards Russell's theory as an attempt to provide an account of the way descriptive phrases actually function in ordinary language, and he compares the kind of analysis of description-sentences effected through the theory of descriptions to a translation from one natural language to another. In both cases, he maintains, "there is more or less explicit and direct appeal to congruence of behavior and linguistic utterance in cognate situations." [3] To test the adequacy of the analysis we simply observe whether the analysans can be substituted for the analysandum without disturbing the normal linguistic behavior of someone familiar with the language. So interpreted, the theory of descriptions is simply a neutral method for replacing one English sentence with another English sentence having a different grammatical form but having the same meaning; here clearly, the question can arise as to whether the proposed translation is correct.

Neither of these interpretations seems to me to reflect precisely Russell's own view. Black's interpretation makes the correctness of the analysis made in accordance with the theory of descriptions depend too much on, what he calls, "sociological" criteria.[4] Russell, I believe, would not regard such criteria as reliable for determining identity of meaning of two linguistic expressions, since he is convinced that ordinary language is vague and ambiguous and users of ordinary language careless and confused in their thought and speech. Pertinent to this point is his reply in *M.P.D.* to Strawson's critique of the theory of descriptions. There he says, concerning his motive for formulating this theory, "... I was concerned to find a more accurate thought to replace

---

[1] Both systems, for instance, would have greater formal simplicity than does ordinary language, in which some phrases of the form "the so-and-so" function as names whereas others do not. In Frege's system *all* descriptions would be interpreted as names; in Russell's *none* would.

[2] In "Russell's Philosophy of Language," *P.B.R.*, pp. 227–255.

[3] *Ibid.*, p. 241.

[4] *Ibid.*, p. 243.

the somewhat confused thoughts which most people at most times have in their heads." [1] Since the theory of descriptions is intended to *correct* some of the ambiguity and vagueness of ordinary linguistic usage, it could hardly appeal to ordinary usage to determine its adequacy.

At the same time, it seems to me correct to say that the theory of descriptions was intended as an analysis of the logical role played by descriptions in ordinary language, and I agree with Professor K. Godel that "Russell does not consider this whole question of the interpretation of descriptions as a matter of mere linguistic conventions, but rather as a question of right and wrong...." [2] That he does regard it as "a question of right and wrong" seems to me evident from the following considerations: In the first place, his criticisms of Meinong and Frege consist, in large part, of a charge that, in different ways, they *fail* to do justice to the way descriptive phrases function in ordinary language; Meinong's because it runs counter to the logical and ontological framework of ordinary language, Frege's because it is "artificial" and does not account for the way descriptive phrases actually function. Secondly, the arguments he presents to show the differences between names and descriptions are based on a consideration of their different logical roles in ordinary language. Finally, his own theory is, as he often says, offered as a technique for *clarifying* description-sentences, for re-stating their meanings in a less confusing way. If this involves a "proposal" of the kind Carnap describes it is not evident how it does so.

I conclude, then, that Russell's aim in formulating his theory of descriptions was to provide an analysis of descriptive phrases that, unlike the analyses offered by Frege and Meinong, delineate the function that descriptions actually have in ordinary language. His purpose, however, was not to duplicate ordinary usage but rather to explicate part of the logical framework which is its foundation. Therefore his suggestion that descriptive phrases can be shown to be, when analyzed in accordance with the formula provided by the theory of descriptions, definitionally eliminable, is not simply a proposal to adopt certain conventions in translating description-sentences. It is, for him, a descriptive account of their logical status in ordinary language. [3]

---

[1] p. 243.

[2] "Russell's Mathematical Logic," *P.B.R.*, p. 130.

[3] Several recent critiques of the theory of descriptions have suggested that it does not do justice to the manifold roles and functions descriptive phrases may have in ordinary language. (Cf. G. E. Moore, *P.B.R.*, pp. 214ff., P. T. Geach, "Russell's Theory of Descriptions," in Margaret MacDonald (ed.) *Philosophy and Analysis* (Oxford, 1954), p. 34; P. E. Strawson, "On Referring," *Mind*, LIX (1950), pp. 320–344.) In only some of its uses, it is suggested, can a descriptive phrase be analyzed in accordance with Russell's formula for translating descrip-

In summary, it may be said that the theory of descriptions is a method of analysis that aims at correcting a logical defect in the structure of ordinary grammar, a defect that is potentially misleading with respect to the structure of reality. It proceeds by eliminating, through contextual definition, an expression which seems to function referentially. Since this expression can be eliminated it is not part of the "minimum vocabulary" needed to describe the ontologically basic features of reality. In a logically perfect language, therefore, no descriptive phrases will appear. These symbols will be (contextually) replaced by symbols for quantifiers, argument and property variables, and logical constants.

It appears, therefore, that although the theory of descriptions was formulated primarily for the purpose of affording insight into the logical structure of description-propositions, it is also a technique for effecting clarification of the ontological presuppositions of these propositions. This question will bear further investigation. Since, however, it is part of a larger issue having to do with the overall relationship between language and reality in Russell's whole reconstructionist program, it can be more fruitfully investigated after I have examined other instances of the method of reconstructionism. I shall examine now a second use of this method, the analysis of class-symbols.

THE ANALYSIS OF CLASS-SYMBOLS

For my purposes the significant development in Russell's analysis of class-symbols was his "no classes" theory, first enunciated in *P.M.*, in which symbols for classes are treated as incomplete symbols. It was this theory which led him to propose a reconstruction of class-sentences [1] that would dispense altogether with class-symbols except as a "symbolic convenience." Before examining this theory, however, it will be helpful to begin by considering briefly the general features of the earlier view of classes to which he subscribed in *P. of M*. His discussion of classes in this work projects some of the fundamental problems that the reconstruction of class-sentences permitted him to resolve, and in so

---

tion-sentences. I shall not discuss these various criticisms, however; I am primarily interested in presenting an account of the essential features of Russell's reconstructionism as a general analytic method. Therefore it would not be particularly apposite to engage in a detailed examination of the theory of descriptions and try to determine the particular respects in which it may or may not be adequate for the purposes for which it was formulated.

[1] I shall use this expression to signify sentences containing class-symbols.

doing illumines the question of why, from his point of view, this reconstruction is desirable.[1]

Russell's entire analysis of classes in *P. of M.* proceeds on the assumption that classes are entities of some sort. The purpose of a philosophical investigation of classes is, he believes, "to indicate the *kind of
object* that is to be called a class." [2] His analysis encompasses two main
points related to this assumption: (1) the relationship between a class
as "one" and a class as "many"; (2) the contradictions generated by
the circumstance that, as entities, classes can be said to be (and also not
to be) members of themselves.

(1) The distinction Russell makes between a class as "one" and as
"many" corresponds to the distinction between an intensional and an
extensional interpretation of classes. According to the former interpretation a class is defined in terms of the class-concept or property that
characterizes each member said to belong to the class. We commonly
say, for instance, that Socrates, Plato, and Aristotle are all *human* or,
indifferently, that they belong to the class *men*. When we interpret a
class in this way, we mark out as the essential feature of the class the
fact that all its members have a common property and hence are a
unified whole, a "one." By contrast, assuming an extensional interpretation a class is defined by an enumeration of its terms, i.e., by listing
the individual members of the class. On this definition, Russell maintains, a class "is more naturally called a *collection*". [3] A collection, he
points out, "is defined by the actual mention of the terms, and the terms
are connected by *and*."[4] "Collection" suggests more adequately than
does the word "class" the aggregate formed by simply listing objects
and connecting them with "and." It seems, for example, somewhat
improper to characterize "Socrates and Plato and Aristotle and ..."
as a *class*, even if, as a matter of fact, they and they alone are designated
by the phrase *all men*. To say that they constitute a *collection* is, of
course, to lay emphasis on the pluralistic aspect of the aggregate they
comprise and interpret this aggregate as essentially a "many."

In order to determine "the kind of object that is to be called a class"

---

[1] In the following discussion I shall not attempt to relate Russell's analysis of class-symbols
to his purely logical interests, even though these may have been, in some obvious sense, his
primary concern. Since I am interested in his analysis simply as an additional instance of
reconstructionism, I shall consider only those aspects of the analysis which have direct bearing
on the ontological (or linguistic-ontological) issue of whether or not class-symbols are genuinely referential.

[2] p. 82. My italics.

[3] *P. of M.*, p. 65.

[4] *Ibid.*

it is necessary to find some way of reconciling these different interpretations, to show that they are not, as they seem to be, incompatible. Russell states the problem raised by this dualistic interpretation as follows: "Is a class which has many terms to be regarded as itself one or many? Taking the class as equivalent simply to the numerical conjunction 'A and B and C and etc.,' it seems plain that it is many; yet it is quite necessary that we should be able to count classes as one each, and we do habitually speak of *a* class. Thus classes would seem to be one in one sense and many in another." [1] In *P. of M.*, however, no real solution to this problem is possible, due to Russell's assumption that classes are entities. The fact that we distinguish between expressions that designate classes as single terms and expressions that denote them as pluralities ("classes of all rational animals," for instance, denotes *the human race* as one term, whereas "all men" denotes it as many) argues, he believes a real difference between the entities these expressions designate, and he concludes that "[we must] infer an ultimate distinction between the class as many and a class as one [and] hold that the many are only many, and not also one." [2] The primary difficulty with such a view, as he himself points out in *P.M.*, is that it would appear to be contradictory to say that classes can be simultaneously one and many. "It there is such an object as a class, it must be in some sense *one* object. Yet it is only of classes that *many* can be predicated. Hence if we admit classes as objects, we must suppose that the same object can be both one and many, which seems impossible." [3]

(2) On the assumption that classes are entities, a class as one may, like any other entity, be itself a member of certain classes. Moreover, in certain cases it is possible to regard a class as one as a member of *itself* as many.[4] This is true quite generally of negative classes, for certainly the class of things that are not, say, teaspoons is itself not a teaspoon and so is a member of itself. In addition, there is at least one positive case in which a class may be said to belong to itself. For if a class is an entity of some kind, then it can be said to be a member of the class consisting of all the entities in the world.[5]

If classes can be members of themselves, this fact is, for mathematical logic, a circumstance of first importance, for it gives rise to Russell's famous paradox concerning classes that are, and also are not, members

[1] *Ibid.*, p. 76.
[2] *Ibid.*
[3] *P.M.*, p. 72n.
[4] *P. of M.*, p. 102.
[5] Cf. *P.L.A.*, p. 261.

of themselves. The following passage shows how this paradox is generated:

If there is any sense in asking whether a class is a member of itself or not, then certainly in all the cases of the ordinary classes of everyday life you find that a class is not a member of itself. Accordingly, that being so, you could go on to make up the class of all those classes that are not members of themselves, and you can ask yourself, when you have done that, is that class a member of itself or is it not?

Let us first suppose that it is a member of itself. In that case it is one of those classes that are not members of themselves, i.e., it is not a member of itself. Let us then suppose that it is not a member of itself. In that case it is not one of those classes that are not members of themselves, i.e., it is a member of itself. Hence, either hypothesis, that it is or that it is not a member of itself, leads to its contradiction. If it is a member of itself, it is not, and if it is not, it is.[1]

We need not consider here the various methods Russell adopted in *P. of M.* and elsewhere, before formulating his "no classes" theory, to avoid this contradiction. It will be sufficient to say that in *P. of M.* he was led to revise his original view that in all cases where there is a class as many, there must also be a class as one. In cases where its existence would lead to a contradiction the class as one is denied.[2] Moreover, the class as many is, he maintains, always of a higher *type* than its members.[3] This theory of types was developed and refined in subsequent works,[4] but his ultimate solution to the problem involved the more radical suggestion that classes are merely "logical fictions" and therefore never exist as genuine objects.

The "no classes" theory is announced, in *P.M.*, in terms that explicitly relate it to the theory of descriptions. "The symbols for classes, like those of descriptions, are, in our system, incomplete symbols; their *uses* are defined, but they themselves are not assumed to mean anything at all. That is to say, the uses of such symbols are so defined that, when the *definiens* is substituted for the *definiendum*, there no longer remains any symbol which could be supposed to represent a class. Thus classes, so far as we introduce them, are merely symbolic or linguistic conveniences, not genuine objects as their members are if they are individuals." [5] In the case of descriptions it was, Russell maintains, possible to

---

[1] *Ibid.*

[2] *P. of M.*, p. 104.

[3] Cf. *Ibid.*, p. 105. See also Appendix B.

[4] See especially his "Mathematical Logic as Based on the Theory of Types," *American Journal of Mathematics*, XXX (1908), 222–262. Reprinted in *L.K.*, pp. 57–102. The theory of types is also discussed in *P.M.*, pp. 37–65.

[5] pp. 71–72.

prove that they are incomplete symbols, but "In the case of classes we do not know of any equally definite proof, though arguments of more or less cogency can be elicited from the ancient problem of the One and the Many." [1] Despite this lack of "proof" it is, he believes – for reasons I shall explain presently – useful to interpret class-symbols as incomplete symbols and thereby dispense with classes as entities.

This is to be accomplished by defining class-symbols in terms of propositional functions, or, rather – since classes can only be defined "in use" – by interpreting *propositions* ostensibly concerning classes as *propositions* concerning propositional functions. Any proposition about a class is to be taken as equivalent to a proposition about a function which defines (or determines) the class. This function stands for the common property, possession of which qualifies an object to be a member of the class in question. Thus the property *human* is a function which is satisfied by Socrates, Plato, Aristotle, etc. In saying that "Socrates is a man," we are not, according to Russell's interpretation, commiting ourselves to the existence of a class *men*; we are simply asserting that Socrates possesses the property of being human. More generally, the proposition "*x* is a (member of the class) *K*" is to be translated as "*x* is a value that satisfies *F*," where *F* is the function that determines *K*. Symbolically this can be expressed as follows: let the expression $\hat{z}(Fz)$ stand for the class determined by *F*. Then $x\sum\hat{z}(Fz)$ will express the membership of *x* in this class. This expression, Russell maintains, may be replaced by the expression *Fx* since, according to the "no classes" theory, $x\sum\hat{z}(Fz) \equiv Fx$.[2] Since statements about classes are equivalent to statements about propositional functions, to say that two classes are *identical* is, for Russell, tantamount to saying that functions which determine them are formally equivalent, i.e., are satisfied by precisely the same set of arguments. Thus the classes *rational animal* and *featherless biped* are identical, despite the fact that their determining functions have a different intension, since anything that is an argument for one is an argument for the other.

With this interpretation the problem of whether classes are best characterized as "one" or "many" is obviated, and the contradiction concerning classes that both are and are not members of themselves is seen to involve a fundamental logical confusion. Classes, as such, are neither one not many. As "logical fictions" they cannot be described as either a unity *or* a plurality. Once it is seen that talk about classes is

---

[1] *Ibid.*, p. 72.
[2] *P.M.*, p. 79.

simply a *façon de parler* it becomes obvious that the question of the
most appropriate way to characterize them simply cannot arise. As for
the contradiction, if symbols for classes are incomplete symbols, then,
Russell maintains, "the whole question whether a class is or is not a
member of itself is nonsense, . . . and . . . it is not even true to say that,
because the whole form of words is just a noise without meaning." [1] If
a proposition about a class is to be significant, it must be capable of
translation into a form in which there is no mention of the class. It must,
as we have seen, be capable of translation into a proposition about
propositional functions and their values. Hoewver, when we attempt to
translate propositions about classes that are (or are not) members of
themselves in accordance with this procedure we find that we cannot
do so. Therefore, they are without significance. In Russell's words:
". . . a proposition about a class is always to be reduced to a statement
about a function which defines the class, *i.e.* about a function which is
satisfied by the members of the class and by no other arguments. . . .
a class . . . cannot . . . significantly be the argument to its defining
functions, that is to say, if we denote by '$\hat{z}(\phi z)$' the classes defined by
ϕz, the symbol '$\phi/\hat{z}(\phi z)/$' must be meaningless. Hence a class neither
satisfies nor does not satisfy its defining function, and therefore . . . is
neither a member of itself nor not a member of itself.' [2]

As I stated above, although Russell did not believe that class-symbols could be proved to be incomplete symbols, he felt that there were,
nevertheless, good reasons for interpreting them as such. Besides en-
abling us to avoid the logical difficulties growing out of the view that
classes are entities, this interpretation will permit us to avoid unnecessary assumptions and will, consequently, narrow the range of possible
logical and ontological error. This point is clearly articulated in the
following passage: ". . . it becomes very difficult to see what [classes]
can be, if they are to be more than symbolic fictions. And if we can
find any way of dealing with them as symbolic fictions, we increase the
logical security of our position, since we avoid the need of assuming that
there are classes without being compelled to make the opposite assumption that there are no classes. We merely abstain from both assumptions.
This is an example of Occam's Razor, namely, 'entities are not to be
multiplied without necessity.' But when we refuse to assert that there
are classes, we must not be supposed to be asserting dogmatically that
there are none. We are merely agnostic as regards them: like LaPlace,

---

[1] *P.L.A.*, p. 261.
[2] *P.M.*, pp. 62–63. Russell is here assuming the validity of the Theory of Types.

we can say, '*je n'ai pas besoin de cette hypothèse.*'" [1] This passage suggests a basic similarity between his motivation for reconstructing class-sentences and his motivation for reconstructing description-sentences. In both cases, it appears, he sought to provide an analysis that would show how we may interpret sentences containing expressions of a certain kind without attributing ontological significance to those expressions. In both cases, he believed, the presence of expressions ostensibly designating entities misleads us into assuming that sentences containing these expressions are about their (supposed) designata and that these entities are, therefore, part of the basic furniture of the world. In order to subvert this assumption, it must be shown that the expressions in question are merely symbolic conveniences without ontological significance. This can be accomplished by demonstrating that they are definitionally eliminable and that, in theory at least, nothing can be stated with them that cannot also be stated without them. Thus there is no need to postulate questionable entities which analysis shows to be unnecessary.

Class symbols, no more than descriptions, are part of the "minimum vocabulary" needed to describe the world; therefore, we need not assume the existence of entities, classes, corresponding to them. As Russell says, ". . . classes cannot be regarded as part of the ultimate furniture of the world. It is difficult to explain precisely what one means by this statement, but one consequence which it implies may be used to elucidate its meaning. If we had a complete symbolic language, with a definition for everything definable, the undefined symbols in this language would represent symbolically what I mean by 'the ultimate furniture of the world.' I am maintaining that no symbols either for "class" in general or for particular classes would be included in this apparatus of undefined symbols." [2]

In the light of Russell's statements in this passage we may consider Professor Urmson's suggestion that, for Russell, to show that class-symbols are incomplete symbols is tantamount to showing that classes do not exist. Urmson argues that in holding such a view Russell is departing from the definition of "incomplete symbol" he had employed in his analysis of descriptions. There, Urmson maintains, to exhibit a symbol as incomplete did not show that the entity supposedly designated by the symbol did not exist but showed "at the most . . . that descriptive expressions were logically eliminable from propositions

[1] *I.M.P.*, p. 184.
[2] *Ibid.*, p. 182.

. . . ." [1] In claiming that exhibiting class-symbols as incomplete would prove that classes do not exist Russell has, Urmson believes, "misrepresented the matter to make it appear that to say of an expression that it was incomplete was inevitably to suggest that it did not stand for any genuine object." [2] Thus, Urmson concludes, "Russell could think of his logical analysis as a metaphysically powerful weapon which enabled him to get down to the basic realities, whereas in fact it merely enabled him to see the mistake in certain logical arguments for admitting as basic entities things which he was rightly reluctant so to regard." [3]

There is, I believe, some confusion on Urmson's part with respect to what Russell means when he relates the "incompleteness" of class-symbols to the non-existence of classes. Urmson apparently assumes that the sense in which the existence or non-existence of classes is at issue in Russell's analysis of class-symbols is what may be termed a *substantive* sense and that Russell is concerned with the question of whether classes "really" exist – as though it were the kind of question that could conceivably be determined through examining the extra-linguistic world. Russell does, admittedly, sometimes speak of the existence of classes in what appears to be a substantive sense. In *P.M.*, for example,[4] he says – in the passage which Urmson uses as the point of departure for his criticism: "It is not necessary for our purposes . . . to assert dogmatically that there are no such things as classes." His real view of the matter, however, is expressed in the passage quoted above, and here, patently, the existence of classes, in a substantive sense of "exist," is not at issue.

What is at issue is the question of whether class-symbols can be eliminated from the propositions in which they occur without changing the meanings of these propositions. Urmson *contrasts* (a) showing that expressions are logically eliminable from propositions and (b) showing that the entities they supposedly designate do not exist. For Russell, however, the only sense in which the non-existence of classes is at issue in his analysis of class-symbols is just this sense, that symbols ostensibly referring to classes are not genuine constituents of the propositions in which they occur. To say that classes do not exist is, for Russell, to say that class-symbols do not function referentially and that, therefore, the facts asserted by class-proposition need not be assumed to contain entities, classes, as elements. This, it seems to me, is precisely analogous

[1] *Philosophical Analysis*, p. 30.
[2] *Ibid.*, p. 31.
[3] *Ibid.*
[4] p. 72.

to the situation with respect to descriptive phrases. In both cases he is arguing from the philosophically clarified form of the proposition to the logical form of the fact the proposition asserts. Since neither descriptions nor class-symbols are indispensable elements in the propositions in which they occur, they cannot be included as part of the primitive notation of a logically perfect language, a language, that is, which "will show at a glance the logical structure of the facts asserted or denied." It is in this sense, and *only* in this sense, that Russell regards his analytic method as "getting down to basic realities."

This concludes my discussion of Russell's analysis of class-symbols. From what we have seen in this section it is clear, I think, that this analysis is sufficiently similar to the theory of descriptions to warrant our categorizing it as an instance of the same general analytic method. I wish to consider now a third, and last, instance of Russell's use of reconstructionism, his logical construction of physical objects.

THE LOGICAL CONSTRUCTION OF PHYSICAL OBJECTS

Russell's logical construction of physical objects is intimately related to his theory of acquaintance discussed in the previous chapter. As we have seen, this theory had its genesis in his assumption that, besides relations (including qualities), only sense-data can be genuinely known. All other entities, or supposed entities, are only "inferred," and for Russell inferred entities are not, strictly speaking, known. This means that the existence of physical objects, qua metaphysical [1] entities, can be called into question, for, so conceived, they are never experienced and, by their very nature, never can be. As he says in the pre-constructionist work, *The Problems of Philosophy*, ". . . if we take any common object of the sort that is supposed to be known by the senses, what the senses *immediately* tell us is not the truth about the object as it is apart from us, but only the truth about certain sense-data which, so far as we can see, depend upon the relations and the object. Thus what we directly see and feel is merely 'appearance' which we believe to be a sign of some 'reality' behind. But if the reality is not what appears, have we means of knowing whether there is any reality at all?" [2]

---

[1] As Russell uses the term, "metaphysical" usually means, roughly, "non-empirical." In *P.L.A.* (p. 272) he says, "By metaphysical entities I mean those things that are supposed to be part of the ultimate constituents of the world, but not to be the kind of thing empirically given – I do not say merely not being itself empirically given, but not being the *kind* of thing that is empirically given."

[2] p. 16.

The difference between our knowledge of sense-data and our knowledge of physical objects (construed as "metaphysical" entities standing "behind" sense-data) is not difficult to see. In the case of a sense-datum the only evidence required to substantiate our belief in its existence is the sense-datum itself. When I say "there is a brown elliptical patch here now" the only evidence needed to establish this statement is my awareness of a brown elliptical sense-datum here now. If I am actually aware of the sense-datum that is the end of the matter; no further evidence is needed. My statement has been completely verified.[1] For Russell, knowledge of physical objects has a quite different status. Knowledge of the existence of a physical object incvolves more than just awareness of sense-data. It involves a belief that there is, in addition to any sense-data we may experience, a non-empirical something that is the "cause" of the sense-data and persists when there are no sense-data at all. Since physical objects (in this sense) can never be given in experience, their existence can only be inferred. The moment this kind of inference enters into a belief, however, the belief becomes less than certain. When I say, for example, "there is a table", I not only assert more than the present empirical evidence can substantiate, I assert more than *any* empirical evidence can substantiate. For at least part of what I mean by "table" is non-empirical and therefore not subject to empirical verification. This is sufficient to render the belief in the table (qua metaphysical entity) questionable, for, Russell insists, "we can never *prove* the existence of things other than ourselves and our experiences."[2]

In *P.P.*, it is true, Russell maintained that though we are never directly aware of physical objects, and therefore can never know them "by acquaintance," we can yet know them "by description" as "the physical object which causes such-and-such sense-data." What is important for the present discussion, however, is not the argument by which Russell tried, in this work, to "save" the common-sense belief in the existence of physical objects. What is important is that through the method of "systematic doubting" he came to the conclusion that the existence of physical objects could be called into question. For it was his assessment of our knowledge of physical objects as doubtful that ultimately led him to attempt to formulate a theory of physical objects not requiring the assumption of an inferred, metaphysical entity.

---

[1] Cf. *O.K.E.W.*, p. 58: "... the immediate facts perceived by sight and touch do not need to be proved by argument, but are completely self-evident."
[2] *P.P.*, p. 22.

There are, I believe, two important aspects of Russell's philosophy directly related to his dissatisfaction with the common-sense notion of physical objects. These are (1) his desire to "justify" physical science and (2) his rejection of postulation.

(1) In saying that Russell desired to "justify" physical science I mean only that he wished to validate its claim to be an empirical undertaking. Just why he thought it necessary to provide a justification of physics is clearly indicated in this passage from *Mysticism and Logic:*

> Physics is said to be an empirical science, based upon observation and experiment.
> It is supposed to be verifiable, i.e., capable of calculating beforehand results subsequently confirmed by observation and experiment.
> What can we learn by observation and experiment?
> Nothing, so far as physics is concerned, except immediate data of sense: certain patches of colour, sounds, tastes, smells, etc., with certain spatio-temporal relations.
> The supposed contents of the physical world are *prima facie* different from these: molecules have no colour, atoms make no noise, electrons have no taste, and corpuscles do not even smell.
> If such objects are to be verified, it must be solely through their relation to sense-data: they must have some kind of correlation with sense-data, and must be verifiable through their correlation alone.[1]

The need for such a justification of physics arises, Russell believes, from the fact that it assumes physical objects as non-empirical entities. Thus if we attempt to correlate physical objects with sense-data in order to verify that they exist, it would seem that verification is not forthcoming. "A correlation can only be ascertained empirically by the correlated objects being constantly *found* together. But in our case, only one term of the correlation, the sensible term, is ever *found*: the other term seems essentially incapable of being found. Therefore, it would seem, the correlation with objects of sense, by which physics was to be verified, is itself utterly and for ever unverifiable." [2]

Since we cannot verify statements about physical objects we must, he maintains, either conclude that physics is not an empirical undertaking or re-formulate the concept of *physical object* in such a way that physical objects are no longer conceived as non-empirical entities standing "behind" sense-data. To effect this re-formulation we must interpret physical objects as "functions of sense-data." ". . . if physics is to be verifiable we are faced with the following problem: Physics exhibits sense-data as functions of physical objects, but verification is only pos-

[1] p. 140.
[2] *Ibid.*

sible if physical objects are exhibited as functions of sense-data. We have therefore to solve the equations giving sense-data in terms of physical objects, so as to make them instead give physical objects in terms of sense-data." [1]

(2) In the first two sections of this chapter I have delineated two instances of Russell's use of Occam's Razor to avoid postulating unnecessary entities. Neither "objects described" nor classes, he believed, need be assumed as part of the ultimate furniture of the world. Since physical objects are never given in sense experience they too are, for him, postulated entities whose existence is problematic. The only entities of whose existence we can be certain are the data of sense. To infer over and beyond these data the existence of entities which somehow "cause" the sense-data is to argument one's ontology without adequate warrant. The presence of physical-object words in the language does not imply the existence of physical objects as ontologically basic entities, any more than the presence of descriptive phrases and class symbols implied the existence of entities corresponding to these expressions. Rather than assume that because there are symbols ostensibly standing for physical objects there must be physical objects, we should try to devise some way of treating physical-object statements as logical functions of sense-datum statements. In this way we can avoid unnecessary and risky inferences to entities not known to exist.

Granting the desirability of exhibiting physical objects as functions of sense-data, what is the procedure we should follow in order to accomplish this? The procedure Russell outlines is quite complex, involving, among other things, construction of a "six-dimensional" space. However, it is not necessary for my purposes to delve into the intricacies of this procedure, since I am here concerned only with the very general features of Russell's logical construction of physical objects, with the *kind* of analysis he is attempting to provide.

It is necessary, first of all, to understand the type of relationship sense-data are supposed to have to physical objects such that the latter can be regarded as a "construction" out of the former. In *O.K.E.W.* Russell suggests that, assuming his interpretation of physical objects, "a 'thing' will be defined as a certain series of aspects, namely those which would commonly be said to be *of* the thing. To say that a certain aspect is an aspect of a certain thing will merely mean that it is one of those which, taken serially, *are* the thing." [2] So characterized, his pro-

---

[1] *Ibid.*, p. 141. Cf. *O.K.E.W.*, pp. 84–85.
[2] p. 85.

cedure for constructing physical objects out of sense-data [1] might seem to be not a "logical" but a "real" construction, with sense-data conceived as *constituents* of physical objects in a way somewhat analogous to the way individual cells make up a bodily organ or atoms make up a molecule. Russell, unfortunately, sometimes speaks in this misleading substantive manner.[2] The way he actually conceives the relationship between sense-data and physical objects is more adequately shown in the statement immediately following the passage just quoted where he says: "Everything will then proceed as before: whatever was verifiable is unchanged, but *our language is so interpreted* as to avoid an unnecessary metaphysical assumption of permanence." [3] It is also shown in his general description of the "method of construction": "Given a set of propositions nominally dealing with the supposed inferred entities, we observe the properties which are required of the supposed entities in order to make these propositions true. By dint of a little logical ingenuity, we then construct some logical function of less hypothetical entities which has the requisite properties. This constructed function we substitute for the supposed inferred entities, and thereby obtain a new and less doubtful interpretation of the body of propositions in question." [4]

From these statements it can be seen that Russell's construction of physical objects is, or is intended to be, a method whereby propositions containing references to physical objects (the "inferred entities") are reconstructed in such a way that, in the propositions as reconstructed, there is no longer any reference to a physical object, but only references to sense-data (the "less hypothetical entities"). These latter propositions, he maintains, will have the same meaning as the original propositions because insofar as the *verifiable content* of the orginal propositions is concerned, nothing has been changed. Since, according to the theory of acquaintance, any word which is significant for us must either designate some entity or entities with which we are acquainted, or be definable in terms of words which designate entities known by acquaintance, it follows that the meaning of physical-object statements must be completely reducible to the sense-datum statements that express their empirical "cash value," i.e., their verifiable content. Anything else physical-object propositions may be supposed to assert must be, ac-

---

[1] The "aspects" are, of course, the sense-data correlated with different points of view from which the "thing" may be observed.

[2] Cf. *M.L.*, p. 138.

[3] *Ibid*. My italics.

[4] *Ibid*., p. 151.

cording to the theory of acquaintance, without significance for us, for it involves something with which we cannot possibly enter into a relationship of acquaintance. For Russell, then, the meaning of a physical-object statement is given in the sense-datum statements that would normally be said to *verify* this statement. Therefore, any physical-object statement can theoretically be re-stated in such a way that all physical-object words are eliminated in favor of words designating sense-data.[1] This is the fundamental precept underlying his logical construction of physical objects.

In order to explicate further this important point, it will be useful to examine an argument advanced by Isaiah Berlin [2] that the meaning of physical-object statements can not be rendered by statements about sense-data. Berlin's argument focuses on the inadequacy of an analysis, in terms of sense-data, of statements about *unobserved* physical objects. In such analyses, he points out, though the physical-object statement is *categorical*, all the sense-datum statements in the analysis of this statement will be *hypothetical*; they will state what sense-data will be obtained *provided* an observer is suitably located. The plain man, however, views with suspicion the replacement of the categorical physical-object statement by hypothetical statements about sense-data that would be obtained under certain conditions; he feels that it substitutes "something intermittent and attenuated for something solid and continuous." [3] Berlin believes that this suspicion of such analyses is well-founded, and he attempts to uncover what it is about them that causes the plain man to distrust them.

He suggests that in order to see just what is wrong with translating a categorical statement about an unobserved physical object into hypothetical sense-datum statements, we must have a clear understanding of the logical differences between categorical and hypothetical statements. Categorical statements, he says, "tend to convey that the object referred to has occurred or is occurring or will occur in time; existed, is existing, or will exist. They have a non-descriptive, existential, ostensive element; they seem to invite us to look for the entity they purport to be about." [4] Hypotheticals, on the other hand, "whatever they describe or mean ... do *not* as a general rule directly assert that some-

---

[1] This does not mean, of course, that sense-datum words can simply *replace* physical- object words. The whole proposition must be recast.

[2] "Empirical Propositions and Hypothetical Statements," *Mind*, LIX (July, 1950), pp. 289–312.

[3] *Ibid.*, p. 290.

[4] *Ibid.*, p. 299.

thing has been, is being, or will be occurring, or existing, or being characterized in some way." [1] Furthermore, "to say that something is occurring 'hypothetically' amounts to saying that it is not, in the ordinary sense, occurring at all, but might or would occur if conditions were realized...." [2]

Berlin maintains that it is this difference between categorical and hypothetical statements with regard to their "existential import" that is the source of the plain man's dissatisfaction with phenomenalistic reductions of physical-objects statements. He is disturbed because he realizes that if the hypothetical sense-datum statements are unfulfilled, if there is no observer suitably located, then there will be no sense-data; and if there are no sense-data then there is, according to the phenomenalistic interpretation, nothing at all. The original statement, however, states something quite different from this. It states that something exists whether or not there are observers "suitably located."

This brings us to the central point in Berlin's criticism of phenomenalistic interpretations of physical-object statements. The mistake phenomenalists make, he maintains, is that instead of giving the *meaning* of physical-object statements (as they claim they are doing) they are describing the conditions under which these statements would be verified, the circumstances in which we should be inclined to *enunciate* the statements. That phenomenalistic analyses do not state the meaning of physical-object statements is proved, Berlin contends, by the following consideration: according to phenomenalists a statement such as "there is a table in the room" is to be analyzed entirely in terms of hypotheticals if no one happens to be observing the table; if someone *is* observing the table, however, this statement must be partially analyzable into categorical propositions about sense-data actually occurring. Now if the phenomenalists were right we would have to admit that the meaning of this statement shifts from partially categorical to wholly hypothetical as we look at and away from the table. Such a view, needless to say, does not square with the ordinary view, which holds that the meaning is the same in both cases – when the table is observed and when it is not. It follows, therefore, that whatever else it may do, a phenomenalistic analysis of physical-object statements does not give the meaning of these statements.

Berlin's criticism of phenomenalism is, I think, an acute one. Not only does he show that (and why) phenomenalistic analyses of existen-

---

[1] *Ibid.*
[2] *Ibid.*, p. 301.

tial physical-object statements do not seem to square with common sense and ordinary language, he also makes the valuable suggestion that phenomenalists may have confused statements which give the meaning of physical-object statements with statements which describe the circumstances under which the physical-object statements would be verified. (I shall call these latter "verificatory statements.") Thus, his criticism gets at what I believe is the all-important question: the relationship between a physical-object statement and its verificatory statements is obviously quite close; but can we say that the latter render the *meaning* of the former?

In Russell's case, at least, I do not think this question can be answered as simply and as straightforwardly as Berlin seems to feel. Berlin rejects phenomenalism because, in his words, it "seems to rest on a mistaken analysis of what normal material object statements state." [1] His whole case against interpreting physical-object statements in terms of sense-datum statements is that to do so is incompatible with the logical and ontological framework of ordinary language. This implies, of course, that an interpretation like Russell's attempts to analyze the ordinary meaning of physical-object statements and is inadequate because it fails to do justice to the ordinary meaning. It seems to me, however, that Russell is not suggesting that his analysis gives the ordinary meaning of physical-object statements, if by "ordinary" we understand the meaning common-sense attributes to them. He realized perfectly well, I think, that for common sense the translation of a physical-object statement into its verificatory sense-datum statements does not duplicate the meaning of the original statement. His point, however, is that the common-sense interpretation of physical-object statements is, for philosophical purposes, unsatisfactory. For it requires that we posit, as referents for physical-object symbols, entities which, on his theory of meaning, we do not and can not know – and therefore can not *mean*.

I have already suggested how, through his adherence to the theory of acquaintance, Russell was led to this theory of meaning. In connection with the present issue – the meaning of statements about unobserved physical objects – the following passage from *O.K.E.W.* is particularly illuminating: "Physics started from the common-sense belief in fairly permanent and fairly rigid bodies – tables and chairs, stones, mountains, the earth and moon and sun. This common-sense belief, it should be noticed, is a piece of audacious metaphysical theorising; objects are not

[1] *Ibid.*, p. 312.

continually present to sensation, and it may be doubted whether they are there when they are not seen or felt." [1] If a statement about an unobserved physical object is interpreted as meaning something *more* than the hypothetical statements about sense-data that would serve to verify the physical-object statement, then physical objects must be conceived as entities which are, to some extent, non-empirical, i.e., "metaphysical." In order to meet the difficulties he felt to be inherent in the notion of physical objects so conceived, Russell suggested a new way of interpreting statements about physical objects. According to this interpretation a statement about a physical object would be just a convenient way of referring to statements about sense-data, actual and possible, and references to physical objects (qua "metaphysical" entities) would fall outside the range of meaningful discourse. Thus according to his interpretation – in contrast to the common sense view – the meaning of a physical-object statement *is* given by its verificatory sense-datum statements.

We cannot conclude, then, that Russell's logical construction of physical objects is just a mistake, a mistake resulting from his failure to understand the logic of physical-object statements in ordinary language. His analysis of physical-object statements as functions of sense-datum statements was intended to provide a *philosophical clarification* of the meanings of such statements, to explicate those aspects of our statements about physical objects that are cognitively significant. It was not offered simply as a description of the ordinary meaning of physical-object statements, but, rather, as an analysis which will improve on the ordinary meaning for philosophical purposes. It does so, Russell believed, because it permits us to define physical-object words in such a way that they need not be assumed to denote entities which, given his view, are not known to exist, but only known entities, sense-data. To the extent that physical-object statements cannot be interpreted as statements about sense-data, to that extent, Russell felt, such statements are without meaning.

We may now see how the logical construction of physical objects would, in theory at least, accomplish the two things he hoped to accomplish by means of it, viz., (1) "justify" physics and (2) enable us to avoid postulation of superfluous entities. (1) As was noted earlier, in order to "justify" physics, we must show that it really is what it claims to be, an *empirical* science. This would be accomplished if we were able to translate physical-object statements into sense-datum statements, for all sense-datum statements are theoretically capable of empirical

[1] p. 82.

verification. And (2) if physical objects are interpreted as logical functions of sense-data, then words ostensibly designating physical objects
are not part of the minimum vocabulary, and statements containing
such symbols need not be interpreted as statements about entities,
physical objects. Therefore, we need not postulate physical objects to
serve as referents of these symbols.

The fundamental similarities between Russell's logical construction
of physical objects and the two instances of reconstructionism previous-
ly discussed are evident. No less than they, it represents an attempt to
avoid entities merely postulated to exist, and it proceeds, as they do,
by reconstructing propositions containing expressions supposedly designating the postulated entities so that in the proposition as reconstructed the expression has been eliminated. In all three cases the reconstruction is supposed to have the same meaning as the original
proposition, and since everything the original proposition states can
be stated without referring to the postulated entities, the expressions
in question are seen to be superfluous. Therefore, though Russell does
not, to my knowledge, speak of them as such, physical-object symbols
are, for him, like descriptions and symbols for classes, "incomplete
symbols," and are not genuine constituents of the propositions in which
they occur. The logical construction of physical objects is, like the
earlier analyses, an instance of his use of Occam's Razor to achieve logical and ontological economy in our speech and thought about the world.
As he says, "... by the principle of Occam's Razor, if the class of appearances will fulfil the purposes for the sake of which the thing was in-
vented by the prehistoric metaphysicians to whom common sense is
due, economy demands that we should identify the thing with the class
of its appearances.... Our procedure here is precisely analogous to that
which has swept away from the philosophy of mathematics the useless
menagerie of metaphysical monsters with which it used to be infested."[1]

CONCLUSION

I have now examined three analyses in which Russell employed
reconstructionism to resolve a philosophical problem. On the basis of
this examination it is possible to make certain summary observations
regarding Russell's use of this method and the results he sought to
achieve by means of it.

In one way or another, the different analyses I have considered all

[1] *M.L.*, pp. 149–150.

aimed at correcting some supposed defect in the grammatical structure of propositions of ordinary language. In each case, Russell believed, the presence of a certain kind of expression distorts the true structure of the proposition in which it occurs. The proposition is *apparently* a proposition about some entity designated by the expression, but, for one or more reasons, the assumption that it is about this entity generates philosophical difficulties. In the case of description-propositions the assumption that descriptive phrases function referentially gives rise to a dilemma concerning vacuous descriptive phrases, culminating in the necessity for assuming the existence of some entity corresponding to such phrases even in order to (truthfully) deny that they exist. In the case of class-propositions, attributing a referential function to class-symbols results in two contradictions: (1) a class must be both "one" and "many" and (2) under certain circumstances a class can be said to be, and also not to be, a member of itself. Finally, in the case of physical-object propositions, a dilemma is occasioned by the fact that if physical-object symbols are assumed to designate (metaphysical) entities, physical objects, then there is an incompatibility between what these propositions presume to assert and what, according to Russell's theory of acquaintance, they *can* meaningfully assert.

Though the problems resulting from the assumption that the expression in question functions referentially are of somewhat different orders,[1] they can all be resolved, Russell believed, in the same general way: by exhibiting the troublesome expression as an incomplete symbol. In order to accomplish this it must be shown that the expression does not appear in a logically clarified restatement of the proposition in which it originally occurs. If it does not, this shows that the expression is not a genuine constituent of the proposition and that no element corresponding to it need be assumed in any fact the proposition may assert (or deny). It is not, therefore, a part of the minimum vocabulary, i.e., not a logically primitive expression *required* for asserting facts of a certain type. Once it is seen that all facts asserted by description-propositions, class-propositions, or physical-object propositions can be asserted without descriptions, class-symbols, or physical-object symbols (respectively), the difficulties to which these expressions give rise disappear.

Reconstructionism, then, is a method which aims at providing philo-

---

[1] It is to be noted, especially, that the problem which led Russell to treat physical objects as logical constructions arose because he was operating with a quite special theory of meaning based on a quite special theory of knowing (a "certainty" theory).

sophical insight into the logical structure of language and the ontological structure of facts. As I pointed out in the previous chapter, Russell assumed a thoroughgoing isomorphism between language and reality and believed that logical and ontological clarification could proceed simultaneously, through the proper analysis of language. Perhaps it is now evident just how this assumption operated in his analytic method. The most important point to bear in mind, in connection with Russell's use of analysis, is that his primary concern in analyzing language was to uncover the basic forms of fact-asserting sentences and the basic expressions required for asserting these facts. In this way he believed he could get at the fundamental reality language is about.

CHAPTER III

CRITIQUE OF RUSSELL'S PHILOSOPHY
OF LANGUAGE

Thus far I have attempted to show the nature, purpose, and uses of Russell's distinctive analytic method, reconstructionism. In the course of my exegesis I have, for the most part, concentrated on simply explicating what seem to me to be salient features of this method and the fundamental assumptions on which it rests. On the basis of the preceding examination I conclude that there are three major assumptions underlying Russell's philosophy of language. In order of increasing importance they are as follows:

(1) The Theory of Acquaintance: all propositions concerning matters of fact are meaningful only to the extent that the (non-syncategorematic) expressions they contain can be defined in terms of expressions standing for entities known by acquaintance. This is my paraphrase of Russell's various statements relating meaning and acquaintance. I believe it is a succinct statemenct of what the theory of acquaintance, consistently applied, amounts to insofar as it has bearing on his philosophy of language.

(2) The Doctrine of Logical Form: there is an isomorphism between facts and the propositions which assert them, such that in a logically perfect language a proposition would "mirror" the structure of the correlative fact.

(3) Philosophical Analysis as Elucidation of Ontological Structure: the ultimate purpose of philosophical analysis is to discover the ontological structure of reality, i.e., to determine the "basic furniture of the world."

I say that these assumptions are in order of increasing importance because each assumption is less comprehensive that the assumption listed after it. (3) fixes the whole course of Russell's approach and determines the uses to which philosophical analysis will be put; (2) determines *how* analysis of language is to proceed, that is, by uncovering the "logical forms" of basic propositions; and (1) determines the specific form the analyses will take. It will be my task in this chapter to examine critically these three assumptions, not only in order to provide a basis for appraising Russell's philosophy of language, but also so that some of the fundamental presuppositions and commitments of recent critics of Russell will themselves be laid bare. I shall examine them in the order in which I have listed them.

THE THEORY OF ACQUAINTANCE

In my discussion of the theory of acquaintance I shall take as my point of departure Max Black's critique of this theory in his essay, "Bertrand Russell's Philosophy of Language." [1] According to Black, Russell's assertion that "We must attach *some* meaning to the words we use, if we are to speak significantly and not utter mere noise, *and the meaning we attach to our words must be something with which we are acquainted*" [2] – this assertion, he maintains, is either an incorrect characterization of the relationship between a word and its meaning, or it involves a new conception of meaning by reference to which the theory of acquaintance is true by definition. In his words, "One of two things must be the case. Either Russell is using the term 'meaning' in one of its customary senses; in that case the argument adduced in favor of the principle is refuted quite simply by pointing out that 'Attila' *means* a certain person with whom we are *not* acquainted in Russell's sense. Or, alternatively, a new sense of meaning is implicitly *introduced* in which only objects with which we are acquainted can be meant by words; in that case the argument is a *petitio principii*." [3] Black points out that underlying the principle of acquaintance is the assumption that "in all genuine knowledge or meaning there must be some ... ultimate fusion of intimacy between the knower and what is known...." [4] But, he argues, it is no more the case that in order to *know* or *mean* something we must have a direct relationship of this type with the object known or meant than it is to be in actual physical contact with a physical object in order to *possess* it. Black allows for the "abstract possibility" that there may be "*independent* grounds for supposing the relationship of *meaning*, unlike that of physical posesssion, to be necessarily direct," [5]

[1] *P.B.R.*, pp. 227–255.
[2] Quoted by Black, *Ibid.*, p. 248. Black's italics.
[3] *Ibid.*, p. 249.
[4] *Ibid.*
[5] *Ibid.*, p. 250.

but it is, he believes, only an abstract possibility, for "neither Russell nor anybody else has yet provided good grounds for believing it to be anything more." [1]

For Russell, we have seen, *meaning* is necessarily a direct relationship because *knowing* is, he believed, necessarily a direct relationship. The intimate connection between meaning and knowing in his philosophy has been shown in Chapter I. There we saw that, for him, the two concepts are related in the following way: all words – excluding "incomplete symbols" and words obviously syncategorematic – designate some type of object, and if a word is to have meaning for us we must have knowledge of this object. Since we can genuinely know only objects with which we are acquainted, it follows that only words standing for objects known by acquaintance are meaningful in the strict sense. Acquaintance is, of course, a direct cognitive relationship; therefore, meaning (in this sense of meaning) is also a direct relationship.

It is patent that Russell's theory of meaning introduces factors that do not ordinarily enter into philosophical accounts of how words mean. In connection with this point it is pertinent to call attention to a statement he makes in his introduction to Wittgenstein's *Tractatus*. There, in the course of enumerating four types of problems that can be raised about language, he says, "Secondly, there is the problem as to what is the relation subsisting between thoughts, words, or sentences, and that which they refer to or mean; this problem belongs to epistemology." [2] In this statement, it is to be noted, Russell characterizes as *epistemological* a problem that is ordinarily regarded as purely *semantical*. Ordinarily the meaning (in the sense of reference) of a word is said to be simply the object the word stands for. Thus, "Attila" refers to, or means, Atilla, and the relation between them is semantical, *not*, certainly, epistemological. Russell argues that "Attila" is really a description, not a genuine name as it is usually taken to be. In so arguing, however, he is clearly conflating two questions that are normally kept distinct: (1) the question of what the word means, and (2) the question of how the word functions for someone who *understands* it. From a purely semantical point of view, of course, the reference of a word has nothing to do with what a particular person understands by that word.

It is not sufficient, however, merely to point out that – and how – Russell's account of meaning, as incorporated into the theory of acquaintance, is at odds with the ordinary conception of meaning. Of more inter-

---

[1] *Ibid.*
[2] p. 7.

est and importance, surely, is the question of the value of the theory of acquaintance, viewed as a tacit recommendation that, for philosophical purposes, we introduce new criteria for determining the meanings of linguistic expressions.

Considered in this light, the theory of acquaintance may be regarded as a claim that the concepts "meaning" and "knowing" are actually more closely related than they are ordinarily taken to be, that they are, in fact, inseparable. For Russell the fusing of the two concepts seemed natural and necessary, for he was convinced that if we are to grasp the true meaning of a linguistic expression, we must see what it comes to when it is translated in terms of items of immediate awareness. This conviction was for him a fundamental commitment, following from his adherence to a Cartesian-type subjectivism and a certainty theory of knowing. For him the traditional conception of meaning leaves out the fundamental aspect of language, namely, its relation to human subjectivity. Unless our basic concepts are related to individual experience they are, he believed, but empty abstractions, literally senseless.

It is important to realize that Russell's suggestion to relate meaning and knowing in this way is not necessarily the result of having *confused* the two concepts. Professor J. W. Reeves has argued that Russell, in his theory of acquaintance, confuses the *meaning* of a proposition with the "facts about my experience that convince me of its truth." [1] This, it seems to me, is an unfortunate way of construing what Russell has done, if only because it makes it appear that once the "confusion" has been pointed out, the issue has been settled: the theory of acquaintance is just a mistake. If we take this course, we may very well miss whatever philosophical insight the theory of acquaintance affords. I have myself suggested that Russell has conflated two different questions about language; but to conflate two questions or two concepts is not necessarily to confuse them. In formulating his theory of acquaintance, Russell was well aware, I believe, that his account of meaning does not preserve the customary distinction between meaning and knowing. But it was, he felt, of philosophical importance to point out a way in which they are, in fact, very closely related. The theory of acquaintance does, of course, reflect the important position epistemological questions occupy in Russell's philosophy of language. And the introduction of epistemological considerations into an account of meaning does result in a theory which may appear to include alien and extraneous elements. But these latter

[1] "Origin and Consequences of the Theory of Descriptions," *Proceedings of the Aristotelian Society*, XXXIV (1933–34), p. 223.

were, for Russell, just the features of his theory which give it an advantage over rival theories from which these elements are missing.

It appears, therefore, that Black is quite correct in suggesting that Russell may have introduced a new sense of meaning, one which makes his argument for the theory of acquaintance, in effect, circular – or, as I should prefer to say, true analytically. But having said this we have not, I believe, come to the fundamental question at issue here. The primary question, it seems to me, is not whether the theory of acquaintance involves circular reasoning, but, rather, whether adopting the theory of meaning by virtue of which it is, in fact, circular is feasible and useful in terms of the purpose for which it was originally proposed. This question can be best approached, I believe, by examining the consequences, for language, of adopting this theory of meaning.

Undoubtedly the most striking consequence – and, for many philosophers, the most bizarre – is that it would establish the meaning of a word as *private* to a particular person. Russell himself was aware of this, asserting, as we have seen, that the vocabulary of the logically perfect language would be "very largely private to one speaker." But under these circumstances would not communication become utterly impossible? Or, at best, a happy accident? Professor Black suggests that with such a language as Russell envisages "The proposition understood by the hearer would not ... be the proposition intended by the speaker. ... communication would be possible only by grace of some kind of pre-established speaker-hearer ambiguity in virtue of which what was a logically proper name for one functioned as a description for the other."[1] This point might appear to be a crucial one for the issue under examination, for supposedly it is the essence of a language to provide a means for communicating, and if any philosophical theory proposes meaning-criteria which would render this impossible, then it would seem that that fact alone should preclude our adopting the theory.

Yet perhaps the question is not so easily settled. Perhaps in thinking that it is the essence of language to provide a means for communicating we have had in mind only the social or pragmatic function of languages. Ordinarily, of course, this is the aspect of language in which we are most interested, since it is this aspect which is most closely associated with everyday life, where language is not subjected to philosophical scrutiny but simply used – to make statements, issue commands, ask questions, etc. The ideal language of which Russell speaks, however, is certainly not intended to be *used* in this sense. In replying to Black's criticism

[1] *P.B.R.*, p. 253.

(just quoted) Russell says, "I have never intended to urge seriously that such a language should be created, except in certain fields and for certain problems."[1] Russell does not specify here what these problems are, but we know from our earlier examination that the primary purpose for which such a language would be developed is nothing less than to provide a symbolic "mirror" of the fundamental structure of reality, a language, that "will show at a glance the logical structure of the facts asserted or denied."

It appears, then, that Russell's conception of a logically perfect language is something very far removed from anything we are accustomed to think of as a language. This being the case, the criticism that this language could not be used for purposes of communication is not as damaging as it at first may have seemed to be, if, indeed, it has any force at all. For since the ideal language of which Russell speaks is not designed to be an instrument for communicating, the fact that it can not be so used is, in itself, of little or no significance.

In the terms of the purely theoretical purpose behind the theory of acquaintance, the primary value of the theory, as I see it, is just the way it draws together two concepts usually kept apart, as though they were completely distinct. Even if we reject Russell's particular view of the relationship between meaning and knowing, it is important to realize that they are, perhaps, as closely related as the suggests. Generally speaking, the objects we claim to know are objects that are somehow "given" to us in the various dimensions of our experience, whether this be sense-experience, value-experience, religious-experience, or whatever. Consequently, if we assume that a particular type of object is the kind of entity that *can* be known we will tend to interpret sentences ostensibly making references to such entities as irreducibly *about* them. If, however, we feel that there is a problem as to the epistemic accessibility of such entities, we will try to reformulate these sentences in such a way that their meaning is stated in terms of other entities, entities which we assume can be known. Or perhaps we will interpret them as not genuinely referential at all. Failing to do either of these things, we will be forced to acknowledge kinds of entities – referents of the words and phrases in the sentences – that we cannot know. But this is to say that though these words and phrases have meaning, *what* they mean is unintelligible. This, it seems to me, is a patent contradiction, and although we may question the particular theory of knowing that led Russell to adopt his theory of acquaintance, I do not see how we

[1] *Ibid.*, p. 694.

can deny the general assumption underlying this theory, the assumption, that is, that the meaning of a sentence must be rendered in terms of entities we can (be said to) know. To the extent that the supposed referent of an ostensibly referring expression cannot be cognized, the expression is vacuous and has no function in the realm of meaningful discourse.

THE DOCTRINE OF LOGICAL FORM

The theory of acquaintance provided Russell with a criterion by reference to which he could ascertain when a proposition in ordinary language has been translated into its final form: the logical form of a proposition is the form the proposition assumes when all of its constituents have been reduced to, defined in terms of, expressions designating objects known by acquaintance. The relationship between the theory of acquaintance and the doctrine of logical form is, therefore, an extremely intimate one in Russell's philosophy. It is to be observed, however, that the soundness of this doctrine is not dependent upon the soundness of the theory of acquaintance; for it is entirely possible both to deny that propositions must have the *particular* form Russell believes they must have, and still maintain that they must be structurally isomorphic with the facts they assert. As such, the doctrine of logical form does not dictate, or presuppose, that a proposition must be expressed in terms of items known by acquaintance. One might grant, for instance, that physical-object symbols or class symbols are perfectly legitimate propositional constituents and still hold that a properly formulated proposition must somehow "mirror" any fact it may assert.

In itself, then, the doctrine of logical form states only that propositions and facts have, in some sense, a common structure, and that a symbolism is more or less adequate depending on the extent to which it does or does not clear exhibit this structure. This conception of the relationship between language and the world has been called into question by many recent philosophers who object to it not because of any difficulties the theory of acquaintance might occasion, but because the quest for logical form is, they believe, a misguided philosophical desideratum. Two major arguments have been raised against the notion of logical form as Russell conceived it. The first argument is that the relationship between language and reality is purely *conventional* and that therefore there is no reason to expect propositions to have any kind of structural similarity with the facts they assert. The second argument is that the "logical form" of a proposition, in the only sense in which that concept is philosophically viable, is the role or function of a sentence, not some inherent "structure" the sentence may possess.[1] In this section I shall examine these arguments and attempt to show what each amounts to as a critique of this fundamental precept of Russell's philosophy of language.

In order to illustrate the kind of charge that has been leveled against the doctrine that language is a symbolic mirror in which the structure of the world is reflected, I shall quote here from a few of the numerous recent philosophical writings in which this doctrine has been impugned:

> There is no need whatsoever for the words used in making a true statement to 'mirror' in any way, however indirect, any feature whatsoever of the situation or event; a statement no more needs, in order to be true, to reproduce the 'multiplicity,' say ,or the 'structure' or 'form' of the reality, than a word needs to be echoic or writing photographic." [2]

> Whatever else Russell is prepared to regard as 'accidental' in language, he is unwilling to abandon the notion that language must 'correspond' to the 'facts,' through one-one correlation of elements and identity of logical structure. But there is no good reason why we should expect language to correspond to, or 'resemble,' the 'world' any more closely than a telescope does the planet which it brings to the astronomer's attention." [3]

> The ... confusion of the logical form of a proposition with the visible form of its expression in a sentence has led to endless confusions. Logicians have sometimes even tried to show that the arrangement of words in a sentence somehow 'pictures,' or corresponds to, the arrangement of 'objects' in the fact to which the sentence refers. They fail. The relation of language to fact is not a simple relation of picture to subject. The grammatical form of any spoken language can only be explained by reference to its history and the accidents of its development.[4]

If the view expressed in these three passages is correct, it would seem to follow that Russell's program of reconstructing propositions in order to clarify their logical forms is quite otiose, since there is no necessity that propositions in any sense "picture" what they are about. Language is not related to reality in the way a picture is related to the object it represents. There is, according to this view, a basic difference between the way a proposition *states* and the way a picture *shows* what it is about. Professor E. Daitz, who discusses this difference at length in her paper, "The Picture Theory of Meaning," [5] summarizes the difference

---

[1] Though the first and second arguments are obviously quite closely related, they are, I think, distinguishable.

[2] J. L. Austin, "Truth", *Proceedings of the Aristotelian Society*, Sup. v. XXIV (1950), p. 119.

[3] M. Black, *P.B.R.*, p. 254.

[4] Stuart Hampshire, "Logical Form," *Proceedings of the Aristotelian Society*, XLVIII (1947–48), pp. 38–39.

[5] In Antony Flew (ed.), *Essays in Conceptual Analysis*, (London, 1956), pp. 53–74.

in this way: "The order of words in a sentence is a conventional order of presentation; the spatial ordering of the elements in a reflection, picture, or map is an iconic order of representation."[1] Daitz' discussion of the differences between stating and showing will help us to see what is fundamentally at issue here, and it will be useful to examine her argument in a little detail.

As a model for sentences, pictures are, Daitz maintains, an unfortunate choice, for there are important differences between the ways pictures and sentences "refer." A picture is an icon: this means (1) that the picture taken as a whole directly represents the object it pictures; (2) that various *elements* of the picture represent, in the same sense, *elements* of the pictured; and (3) that the arrangement of elements of the picture directly shows the arrangement of the elements of the pictured. It follows from this that there must be one and only one element of the picture for each element of the object pictured, and that these elements must be related in similar ways in both the picture and the object pictured. That is to say, there must be a complete structural isomorphism between the picture and that of which it is a copy. This is what is meant by saying that a picture *shows* what it is about.

A sentence, however, does not function in this way. It "does not signify because it is a pattern of marks – its physical appearance is irrelevant in the sense that there is no correlation between appearance and function." [2] This is simply to say that a sentence is not an icon. Whereas it is the essence of an icon to *show*, it is the essence of a sentence to *state*. As Daitz says, "It is clear that sentences do not show, but state, that arrangement, which is an essential factor in iconic signification, need not occur in conventional signification, that the elements of a sentence do not stand for objects but (may be used to) refer to or describe objects. And since the words in a sentence do not stand for objects, they cannot be in correspondence, let alone one to one correspondence, with objects." [3] Therefore, Daitz concludes, "A sentence and a picture differ in the very respects in which – if the one is to be a model for the other – they would have to resemble one another." [4]

Let us now attempt to see just what bearing this conclusion – that sentences are not icons – has on Russell's conception of logical form. It is immediately evident that so far as *ordinary language* is concerned, it is manifestly true that, in the usual sense of the word, sentences do

---

[1] p. 63.
[2] p. 66.
[3] p. 67.
[4] *Ibid.*

not "picture" the facts they assert. They are capable of referring to these facts not because they duplicate their structure but because there exist linguistic conventions which simply *tie* certain locutions to certain facts. There is little or nothing in the visible form of its expression which indicates a structural similarity between a sentence in ordinary language and the fact it asserts. So far from denying this, however, Russell was at pains to point out that this is the case; indeed, it is just this aspect of ordinary language which he, qua philosopher, was most concerned about. For it is, he believed, the *failure* of sentences in ordinary language to show clearly the structure of the facts corresponding to them that is the source of many false notions concerning the ultimate nature of reality. Sentences in ordinary language do manage to assert facts without, in any obvious sense, picturing these facts, and for ordinary purposes it is certainly not necessary that they do so. For ordinary purposes statements such as "The author of Waverley is Scotch," "Socrates is a man," and "There is a book on the desk" – all of which, according to Russell, are inadequately formulated – are quite serviceable. We all understand, in a perfectly legitimate sense of "understand,' what these sentences are about. Granted, then, that for ordinary purposes, "there is no need whatsoever for the words used in making a true statement to 'mirror' in any way ... any feature whatsoever of the situation or event ..." – granted this, what bearing does this fact have on the quest for logical form as a *philosophical* enterprise? The answer to this question, I believe, is that if it has any bearing at all it has very little. What is, or is not, required of language for ordinary purposes was of little interest to Russell, for the simple reason that this aspect or dimension of language was not, for him, the philosophically important one. What *is* philosophically significant about language is what it reveals – or can be made to reveal – about the nature and structure of facts, especially what it reveals about the *basic constituents* of facts. Most propositions of ordinary language, however, do not clearly show the basic constituents of the facts corresponding to them, and they frequently mislead us if we attempt to use them as a basis for making inferences about the world. In order to forestall such false inferences the propositions must be reconstructed so that the basic constituents can be clearly seen. It is in this sense, and only in this sense, that a philosophically clarified proposition can be said to "picture" a fact.

It is obvious, then, that in claiming that language, even philosophically clarified language, should "picture" reality, Russell does not mean that a (true) proposition is a picture of a fact in the same sense that, say, a Constable landscape is a picture of a portion of the English countryside. Though he does try to show a connection between showing and stating that is usually overlooked – viz., that sentences can be formulated in such a way as to show more explicitly the constituents of the facts they state – he certainly does not think that stating is, *simpliciter*, the same thing as showing. Obviously, no sentence, not even a sentence in a logically perfect language, can duplicate the structure of a fact in the iconic way a picture duplicates the object it pictures; and the relationship between language and reality is not, as Russell certainly realized, "a simple relation of picture to subject." The metaphor of language as a picture is, after all, only a metaphor. Its usefulness for Russell was tied up with his whole conception of linguistic analysis as a means for getting at the ontological structure of reality. For those philosophers who have no such goal, and who regard analysis of language as a philosophical end in itself, there is no reason to insist on, or look for, any kind of structural similarity between language and reality; and it is not surprising that they would see no more resemblance between language and reality than there is between "a telescope [and] the planet which it brings to the astronomer's attention." For Russell, however, it is imperative that we uncover those features of our language which have a counterpart in the extra-linguistic world and separate them from those that do not. That analysis of language can provide ontological insight is, of course, an assumption – it is, indeed, Russell's fundamental assumption. And this assumption can, of course, be called into question. This, however, is another question, one which I shall examine at a later time. For my present purpose it is, I think, sufficient to have shown why Russell's doctrine of logical form cannot be dismissed simply by calling attention to the conventional (non-pictorial) character of the language we use, and quite successfully use, for purposes of ordinary communication.

There is, however, another, perhaps more serious, objection to Russell's view of language as a kind of picture of reality. This is the argument that it results, ultimately, from confusing *meaning* with *reference*. In essence, the objection to this theory of meaning and its concomitant doctrine of logical form states, following the dictates of the later Wittgenstein, that language is a "tool," the meaning-dimension of which is closely associated with the particular linguistic task it is used to accomplish. Russell's mistake, it is claimed, is that he confused meaning with reference and thus tended to focus his attention on only one particular use of language, the referring use; consequently he thought of linguistic expressions as somehow meaning the entities they are used to refer to. Against this view of language it is argued that the meaning of a word or phrase is never the referent of that word or phrase, but is, rather, the set of rules that govern its use. As Strawson puts it, "For a ... referring expression to have a meaning, it suffices that it should be possible in suitable circumstances to use it to refer to some one thing, person, place &c. Its meaning is the set of linguistic conventions governing its correct use so to refer.... Sentences and phrases and words have meanings, in virtue of which they may be used to make statements and to refer to things. But the meanings of sentences are not the statements they are used to make, and the meanings of words and phrases are not the things they are used to refer to. Only the grossest equivocation with words like 'mean' and 'refer' can continue to obscure these facts." [1] It is to be noted that Strawson distinguishes here between a *sentence* and a *statement*. Elsewhere he makes a similar distinction between an expression and a use of an expression.[2] For the theory of meaning to which he subscribes – which I shall call the "use-theory" – these distinctions are of fundamental importance. Concerning the sentence-statement distinction he says, "One must distinguish between what can be said about the *sentence*, and what can be said about the statements made, on different occasions, by the use of the sentence. It is about statements only that the question of truth or falsity can arise; and about these it can sometimes fail to arise."[3]

According to the use-theory of meaning a sentence in no sense pictures reality. Indeed, the very conception of what a sentence is has changed. For Russell a sentence is a kind of linguistic complex made up of names (standing for particulars) and relation-words (themselves a kind of name) which, if true, corresponds to a fact in the world. According to the use-theory, however, a sentence is construed as an instrument for accomplishing a certain linguistic task. Sentences may be used to assert facts, but they are used for a variety of other purposes as well: for giving commands, expressing wishes or beliefs, for making promises, and so on. Moreover, even when sentences are used assertively, one and the same sentence may be used to make statements having quite different logical forms. Strawson points out, for instance, that the sentence "The cat is a hunter" can be used to make a statement about an individual cat as well as a generalization about cats. And Black, main-

---

[1] *Introduction to Logical Theory*, (London, 1952), pp. 188–189.
[2] Cf. "On Referring," in *Essays in Conceptual Analysis*, p. 27.
[3] *Introduction to Logical Theory*, p. 175.

taining that "every form of words may express several different propositions according to context," cites no less than eight different assertions the sentence, "This is a white mantlepiece," can be used to make. [1] The meaning of a sentence is still conceived as a function of the meanings of the several words that go to make it up, but whereas for Russell sentence-meanings stand to word-meanings analogously to the way a picture, taken as a whole, stands to the various parts of the picture, according to the use-theory, word-meanings stand to sentence-meanings in a quite different way; as, in Ryle's words, "the tennis-racket stands to the strokes which are or may be made with it." [2] Such a conception of meaning, clearly, focuses attention on the pragmatic dimension of language, the way language functions in actual use-situations. Word-meanings are said to contribute to the total meaning of the sentence by making it possible to use the sentence to perform certain linguistic acts, acts it could not be used to perform if it were differently constituted; just as a tennis racket could not be used to make the strokes it *can* be used to make if it did not have particular size, shape, and material composition it does have. Consequently, in the only sense in which a sentence can be said to have "logical form" it has not one form but several, for it can be used for several different linguistic purposes.

The emphasis that has been placed on the pragmatic dimension of language by philosophers who subscribe to the use-theory of meaning has been, in certain respects and for certain purposes,[3] quite salutary. It has resulted in an increased sensitivity to the subtleties of ordinary usage and to the dangers involved in trying to force different linguistic forms into a particular mold. Nevertheless, it seems to me that in their haste to comply with Wittgenstein's mandate, "Don't look for the meaning, look for the use," many philosophers have actually tried to assimilate meaning to use and have, consequently, under-emphasized, if not ignored, the *semantic* dimension of language. Let us see how this is so.

First of all, it should be pointed out that distinguishing between a *sentence* and a *statement* and between an expression and a *use* of an expression would necessitate a revision in some of our customary ways of

---

[1] *The Nature of Mathematics*, (New York, 1933), p. 30. For Black the differences arise from the different questions the sentence may be used to answer.

[2] "The Theory of Meaning," p. 249.

[3] This emphasis is, I believe, closely related to, perhaps to a large extent a consequence of, the conception of linguistic analysis as a kind of "therapy." I shall examine this question in the next section.

speaking about language. For instance, instead of saying, "The sentence 'Socrates loves Plato' states a relationship between Socrates and Plato," we would have to say, "The sentence 'Socrates loves Plato' *can be used to state* a relationship between two persons, one named 'Socrates' and the other named 'Plato.'" This formulation may seem somewhat artificial, but it is, according to Strawson's requirements, strictly correct, since not only does a sentence not itself state – but is only *used* to state – but expressions, even proper names, do not refer, but are only used to refer.[1] This example, however, perhaps conceals the benefits which accrue from employing these distinctions and may suggest that the use-theory is the epitome of philosophical preciosity. The value of distinguishing between sentences and statements and between expressions and uses of expressions is seen to better advantage by applying them in the case of a sentence such as "The cat is a hunter." In this case these distinctions make it possible to say that the *sentence*, "The cat is a hunter," can be used to make a statement about cats, taken as a class, or to state something about a particular cat. This permits us to say that the sentence has a definite meaning – there is a set of conventions which permits us to use it to make either statement – without committing ourselves to saying that it *refers* either to the class *cat* or to a particular cat.

But useful though it may be for certain purposes, there is something about the use-theory that suggests linguistic legerdemain. If we ask, "What does the sentence 'S' mean?" we are told, in effect: "The question is inappropriate; the proper question is, rather, '*How* does the sentence 'S' mean?' And the answer to this question is that it means by virtue of certain 'linguistic conventions governing its correct use.'" This response seems somehow to have missed the point of our question. It is, as it were, on a different level from our question. The difficulty, clearly, is that whereas we were asking, or trying to ask, "What fact or state of affairs does the sentence 'S' assert?" we were interpreted as asking, "What is it, in virtue of which the sentence can be legitimately employed to make assertions of a cerain type?" How, then, can we ask what we are trying to ask, namely, to what state of affairs does this set of words (whether it be called "sentence," "statement," "proposition," or whatever) refer? When I ask, for example, "What is meant by the sentence, 'Caesar crossed the Rubicon,'?" I normally wish to know what precise state of affairs, if any, this group of words asserts. And if it be answered that the meaning of the sentence must be given in terms of

---

[1] Cf. "On Referring," p. 47.

linguistic rules and conventions and not in terms of extra-linguistic facts, then I can only attempt to rephrase my question until I have hit upon a locution that will satisfactorily convey what I wish to ask.

What this shows, I think, is that the use-theory does not satisfactorily accomodate the semantical use of "mean." Philosophers who adhere to a thoroughgoing use-theory are, it seems to me, dominated by the "tool" metaphor quite as completely as Russell was dominated by the "picture" metaphor. So dominated by it are they that they apparently do not recognize the fundamental importance for language of its semantic dimension. That it is of fundamental importance is attested to by the fact that, to a very great extent, the possibility of there being a pragmatic sense of meaning at all is contingent on there being meaning in the semantic sense. It is no doubt true that an expression or a sentence may function in different ways in different contexts, in different language-games. What it is essential to realize, however, is that in order to have any linguistic function at all, expressions and sentences must have a *referential* use, i.e., it must be possible to state *what* it is that they refer to. *Whatever* the purpose of our language may be, whether it be to inform, command, amuse, or anything else, we are unable to accomplish this purpose unless the expressions in our statements, commands, jokes, etc. have a referring use which the other uses *presuppose*. No matter how many different uses a given locution may have, it says nothing unless the (non-syncategorematic) expressions which go to make it up have a referring use. This, I take it, becomes evident once it is pointed out; and it shows, I think, that we cannot treat language as though it were *simply* a tool, *simply* an instrument for accomplishing certain linguistic tasks.

The relevance of this fact for our discussion of logical form is that it shows that we must, somewhere, permit the semantic, referential dimension of language to have a role, and a fundamental role, in determining linguistic forms. Since language is *basically* referential, it is futile to try to ignore, or minimize, the part the semantic dimension plays in determining its forms. If it is necessary to do so we may surrender *sentences* to the use-theory; little will be lost in doing so, since we may retain *statements* as the bearers of logical form in the semantical sense. Now, instead of saying, "The sentence 'S' has such and such a form," we shall say, " 'S' asserts a statement which has such and such a form." And we shall speak of the constituents of the *statement* as designating constituents in the corresponding fact. And finally, we shall speak of the form of the *statement* as "picturing" the form of the fact it asserts. This may well be, after all, a more precise way to describe what we really intended all along. The important point is that the semantic dimension is retained and acknowledged, as, on any adequate theory of language, it must be.

I conclude, therefore, that though the reference-theory of meaning to which Russell subscribed was, to some extent, perhaps, based on an overly simple conception of the myriad tasks language can be used to perform, the emphasis he placed on the referential aspect of language is, for the most part, justified. Consequently the doctrine of logical form which rests on this theory of meaning does not appear to be vulnerable to the criticism that it results from a confusion of meaning with reference. Meaning, in the fundamental sense, *is* reference.

It might be maintained, however, that even putting all other criticisms of Russell's philosophy of language to one side, there is still the problem that it is premised on a most questionable assumption about the philosophical *purpose* of linguistic analysis. This assumption, we have seen, was that the purpose of such analysis is, in some sense, to elucidate the structure of reality. The question we must now examine is: in precisely what sense is analysis of language capable of providing us with insight into ontological structure?

PHILOSOPHICAL ANALYSIS AS ELUCIDATION
OF ONTOLOGICAL STRUCTURE

In our critique of Russell's philosophy of language we have now arrived at the most far-reaching of the several important theses which gave to his program of analysis its distinctive form. The assumption that philosophical analysis of language aims at elucidating the basic structure of reality shaped his entire approach to linguistic analysis and led him to conclude that rescontructionism – the explication of logical form – is the analytic technique appropriate for effecting *philosophical* clarification of language.

It is a widely held view among Anglo-American philosophers that analysis of the type advocated by Russell is, if not futile, then certainly extremely limited in what it can accomplish. Russell's conception of analysis is, it is felt, too rigidly reductionistic, and is, withal, incapable of dealing with the complex philosophical problems associated with the myriad aspects of ordinary language. To a certain extent this criticism has been seen already, in the previous discussion of his notion of logical form. What we must see now is that (and how) it arises out of a quite different conception of the *purpose* of philosophical analysis.

We may begin by noting Professor Weitz' description of the change that has taken place in English philosophy from Russell (by which he means the Russell of the logical atomist period) until the present. Weitz describes this change as "the shift from the belief that the prime task of philosophy is the replacement of castigated expressions by good ones, to the belief that this task is the elucidation of expressions, such as they are." [1] This characterization does not, unfortunately, mention the ontological aspect of Russell's views about analysis – an aspect that is all too frequently overlooked – but for the present we may let this pass. What I am interested in now is the fact that many contemporary philosophers of analysis take the primary task of philosophy to be "the elucidation of expressions, such as they are." This conception of philosophy derives, obviously, from Wittgenstein, and it has its roots in the firm conviction that philosophy is, as he maintained, a kind of "therapy." Let us see what this involves.

For Wittgenstein philosophy is, essentially, an activity; not, as it has usually been thought to be, a theory (or a collection of theories). There are no distinctively philosophical questions, in the sense of questions that have a *subject-matter* peculiar to philosophy. Philosophy is a method, or a set of methods, by means of which we get clear about the "logic of our language." [2] Philosophical problems are those generated by a failure to grasp the true form or function of certain kinds of propositions. In the *Tractatus* Wittgenstein was primarily concerned with one particular type of proposition, the assertive type, and believed that most linguistic confusions – or at least those of most interest to philosophers – were due to a failure to get clear about the way such propositions function. In particular, he was concerned with those confusions arising from a failure to realize that certain propositions, ostensibly assertive, actually transcend the "limits of language" and so are senseless. In his later writings, however, especially in the *Philosophical Investigations*, he came to feel that linguistic confusions of the sort that are of philosophical interest occur in connection with almost every conceivable type of proposition. Indeed, so pervasive is this confusion that nothing less than a detailed analysis of the functions of words in all the numerous language-games that go to make up the rich, variegated structure that is human language will

[1] "Oxford Philosophy," *Philosophical Review*, LXII (1953), p. 228.
[2] Cf. *Tractatus*, 4.003.

suffice to dispel it. Both in the *Tractatus* and in the *Philosophical Investigations*, however, the aim of philosophizing is, I believe, essentially the same: to show us how to disentangle ourselves from linguistic confusion. Philosophy must show clearly the conceptual paths we are to follow if we are to avoid "the bewitchment of our intelligence by means of language." [1]

This conception of philosophy as "therapy" is, in itself, arresting enough. What is really revolutionary about Wittgenstein's thesis, however, is his view that those who are in most need of the kind of therapy philosophy provides are none other than philosophers themselves. In one of his most striking metaphors, he characterizes philosophers as "savages," saying, "When we do philosophy we are like savages, primitive people who hear the expressions of civilised men, put a false interpretation on them, and then draw queer conclusions from it." [2] Philosophy, then, is both patient and physician, and the patient, it would seem, is extremely vulnerable to illness. The physician, the therapeutic philosopher, must, consequently, bring all his analytic skills to bear, not only to cure the patient, but also to protect him from subsequent illnesses. This he does by sedulously acquainting him with the complexities of the various languages game and making him aware of the way language functions in each. Assuming this can be accomplished, there is no reason to believe the patient will not become healthy and remain so.

If the Wittgensteinian thesis is correct, philosophical problems are not genuine problems; they are pseudo-problems generated by philosophers' own confusions about language. The language itself, it is to be noted, is not at fault; the fault is, rather, with philosophers who insist on drawing "queer conclusions" about the forms and functions of certain types of propositions.

In the *Philosophical Investigations* the task of philosophy is conceived as a kind of "linguistic phenomenology," the main function of which is to provide a purely descriptive account of the rules or "paradigms" operative in the various language games. "Philosophy may in no way interfere with the actual use of language; it can in the end only describe it." [3] Always in our philosophical investigations of language we must ask: "... how is this sentence applied – that is, in our everyday language? For I got it from there and nowhere else." [4]

It is against this Wittgensteinian backdrop that the conception of

---

[1] *Philosophical Investigations*, (New York, 1953), p. 47.
[2] *Remarks on the Foundation of Mathematics* (Oxford, 1956), p. 39.
[3] p. 49.
[4] p. 51.

philosophical analysis adhered to by many of Russell's present-day critics is to be scrutinized. Commitment to the thesis that philosophy is a kind of therapy is, I think, responsible for the assumption that the primary task of philosophy is "the elucidation of expressions, such as they are." For if the purpose of philosophy is simply to correct linguistic confusions, then, as Wittgenstein insisted, we need but point out the proper function of the confusion-producing expressions. Having done so, the philosophical task is completed. There is no question of *reforming* language, of "replacing castigated expressions by good ones." As Strawson says, ". . . for the old, limited and theory-ridden program of analysis, we are to substitute a different aim: that of coming to understand philosophically puzzling concepts by carefully and accurately noting the ways in which the related linguistic expressions are actually used in discourse." [1]

The question we must now consider is whether the Wittgensteinian conception of analysis is, in itself, adequate; whether, that is, it is sufficient to resolve all problems that may be of interest to philosophers. This amounts to asking whether there are philosophical problems that are not generated by some kind of linguistic *confusion* and are not, therefore, "pseudo-problems." If there are no other philosophical problems than these, then the type of analysis practiced by Russell is, for the most part, superfluous and his program of reconstructionism misguided.

In attempting to answer this question I think we must admit at the outset that analysis of the therapeutic kind is extremely valuable technique for shedding light on a great many problems that have perenially plagued philosophers. It has shown some of these to be mere pseudo-problems and, perhaps more importantly, it has shown the necessity for re-formulating a great many others. By extricating us from conceptual tangles, by breaking spells that certain linguistic models have had over us, therapeutic analysis makes it possible for us to gain an entirely new perspective on certain kinds of philosophical problems. It therefore leads to genuine philosophical insight.

Nevertheless, there is, I submit, more to philosophical analysis than breaking spells or disentangling concepts, however important these activities may be. The therapeutic type of analyses is, I believe, important primarily as a *preliminary* activity, necessary in that it clarifies what, precisely, the philosophical issue in any patricular case actually is. It is one of the most significant contributions of this activity that it

[1] *The Revolution in Philosophy*, p. 104.

sometimes is able to show that once the issue has been clearly stated the problem it supposedly involved completely disappears. But it would be a mistake to assume that this always occurs and that, if the problem does not disappear, the issue has simply not been properly clarified.

Though there are almost certainly others, there is, it seems to me, at least one fundamental philosophical question to which the therapeutic type of analysis fails to provide an answer; indeed, it is not the kind of question which could even arise within the framework of therapeutic analysis. This is the question: what are the basic ontological assumptions embedded in the categorial matrix of ordinary language? This is not a question which ever arises for the therapeutic analyst simply because it is not a question that concerns the *use* of language. It is, rather, a question concerning, in the most fundamental sense, its *reference*, its semantic dimension. From the point of view of therapeutic analysis the important aspect of language is its pragmatic aspect, how it is used within a particular language-game. For instance, in the previous section it was observed that the expression "the cat" can be used in at least two different ways, to *refer* to an individual cat and to *refer* to the class *cat*. This, for therapeutic analysis, is the only type of consideration that is of philosophical significance – the actual use of an expression. I wish to suggest, however, that after these – and other – uses have been pointed out, after the function of the expression in every conceivable context has been noted, there still remains the question: what is *meant* in saying that the expression "the cat" may be used to refer to an individual or to a class? Are we, in saying this, committing ourselves to the existence of entities, *individuals* and *classes*? If not, to what do we commit ourselves when we speak of individuals and classes? And, in general, *to what kinds of entities do our forms of speech commit us?*

Russell's philosophy of language, as I interpret it, represents an attempt to provide a procedure whereby this question can be answered. In order to elucidate the nature of the commitment which our use of certain kinds of propositions involves us in, he sought to translate these into another form. These propositions were of a type containing expressions ostensibly designating a particular category of objects; and if, on being translated, these expressions were seen to be eliminable, this indicated that the original proposition did not involve us in an ontological commitment to the category of objects in question. The real ontological commitment it involved was shown by expressions present in the proposition as translated; unless, of course, these expressions could also be eliminated by an analogous re-formulation. Expressions remaining in these final translations directly designate the kinds of entities to whose existence our use of the original proposition commits us.

It seems to me obvious that the investigation of the ontological commitments of ordinary language is a matter of interest and importance to philosophers and is an investigation that remains after therapeutic analysis has done its job. But I shall not argue these points further. What I wish to point out at this time is that it was Russell's use of analysis for the purpose of carrying out such an investigation that led him to pursue a policy of "replacing castigated expressions by good ones." This point is apparently lost on some of his critics who, assuming that his is approximately the same task as theirs – elucidation of the various rules and paradigms of different language-games – deprecate the use of reconstructionism as an analytic technique. Strawson, for instance, asks, "Why should it be supposed that the only way to gain an understanding of the words which express the philosophically puzzling concepts was to translate sentences in which they occurred into sentences in which they did not occur? ... It is too turgid a conception of analysis, because it supposes the existence of exact quasi-definitional relations between classes of concepts, which do not in fact obtain. It is too narrow, because it neglects altogether very many quite different features of the functioning of language, which it is of the first importance accurately to note and describe, if our philosophical problems are to be resolved." [1] Though this passage is not intended as a criticism of Russell in particular, he is one of the chief proponents of the type of analysis Strawson is here impugning. To this criticism it is perhaps sufficient to reply that, so far as Russell's method of analysis is concerned, it certainly was not intended to be a technique for explicating all the "different features of the functioning of language." Rather, it was intended to clarify ordinary language as a vehicle for exhibiting the ontological structure of the world. Consequently Strawson's remarks here have little force as a criticism of Russell's philosophy of language, since they fail to relate his reconstructionism to the main problem it was designed to solve.

Granting, then, that Russell's attempt to elucidate ontological structure is a legitimate and valuable quest – one for which the methods of therapeutic analysis are not adequate – we must now examine two fundamental, and closely related, questions about his philosophy of language. These are (1) *in what sense* does clarification of logical structure result in clarification of ontological structure? and (2) what are the

[1] *Ibid.*

criteria by reference to which we can ascertain when a proposition of ordinary language has been properly clarified?

(1) In order to see how clarification of ordinary language will, according to Russell, provide us with knowledge of ontological structure, we must examine the salient features of the ideal language he envisages. As we have seen, one of the most important features of this language is that it will contain no expressions designating "non-basic" entities. This means that unlike unclarified ordinary language it will be purged of all those expressions which seem to refer to entities of some type or other but actually do not. This, then, is one of the ways in which clarification of the structure of ordinary language reveals ontological structure – in the negative sense that it shows how many *fewer* entities, or types of entities, there are in the world than we might suppose on the basis of an uncritical interpretation of the propositions of ordinary language. The world does not contain numbers, or golden mountains, or classes, or physical objects, or a variety of other things we sometimes assume it contains. Expressions ostensibly designating such entities are merely incomplete symbols having no ontological significance. What it does contain – and this is the other way in which clarified ordinary language can be said to exhibit the structure of the world – is shown in the vocabulary of the ideal language. Here we find the "minimum vocabulary" needed for saying everything we wish to say about the world. The objects designated by expressions in this vocabulary are the essential elements, the "atoms," which must be supposed to exist in order for the words in our language to have the meaning they have.

(2) If it is the case that the vocabulary remaining after ordinary language has been purged of its incomplete symbols represents the basic entities in the world, the crucial question, patently, is how we are to determine *when* ordinary language has been properly clarified, so that we may read off the structure of reality from the structure of the ideal language. Unfortunately Russell has not explicitly stated the criteria to be invoked in order to determine when a proposition in ordinary language can be said to be clarified, but on the basis of our previous examination of his uses of reconstructionism we may conclude that there were three such criteria.

In the first place, there was, in each instance of his use of this method, a problem which gave rise to a need for the reconstruction. In the case of the theory of descriptions there was a problem concerning, especially, vacuous descriptive phrases. In the case of the analysis of class-symbols there was a problem concerning the class as one and the class as many, as well as a problem having to do with classes that are, and are not, members of themselves. And in the case of the logical construction of physical objects there was a problem concerning the "metaphysical" status of physical objects. In all of these cases, reconstructionism was employed to correct the linguistic situation giving rise to the particular problem. Therefore, it seems safe to say that for Russell it is a minimal requirement that clarification of a proposition of ordinary language succeed in eliminating any conceptual puzzels or problems which the presence of a certain type of expression in the proposition may generate.

Secondly, Russell believed that clarification of ordinary language must proceed on the basis of his fundamental maxim that "Whenever possible, logical constructions are to be substituted for inferred entities." By "inferred entities" he meant those whose existence is suspect because they are not known with (what he considered) sufficient certainty. The maxim is, then, a heuristic device for ascerting what expressions ostensibly designating such entities amount to when defined in terms of expressions referring to relatively less problematic entities. Such a definition will, he believed, disclose what the original expressions really mean.

Russell's third criterion – and this is, in a sense, only a particular form of the second – was that the *final* translation of a sentence must contain only expressions designating objects known by acquaintance. Only when defined in terms of such objects can it be seen what our words really mean. The *ultimate* test of whether propositions are properly clarified is whether they contain expressions other than those designating objects known by acquaintance.

In connection with this third criterion an issue of fundamental importance must now be raised. We have seen that Russell's reconstructionism attempts to elucidate ontological structure in two ways: (1) by eliminating incomplete symbols; (2) by showing what expressions in our language come to when they are defined in terms of objects known by acquaintance. It seems, however, that these two types of clarification are, at bottom, identical. For in the last analysis all expressions *except* those designating objects known by acquaintance are incomplete symbols. A great deal of clarification is possible without invoking the principle of acquaintance – we may, for example, dispense with descriptive phrases and class symbols – but this produces only *relative* clarity and so permits only a partial insight into ontological structure. It appears, then, that, for Russell, reconstruction of ordinary language *must* proceed in a particular direction and *must* terminate in a particular "picture" of the structure of reality. In the end the basic expressions *must* designate objects of acquaintance. But if it can only proceed in accordance with a preconceived notion of what the world must be like, then Russell's program of clarifying ontological structure is, it would seem, *circular* and elucidates the structure of reality only in the rather Pickwickian sense that it shows what the world is like (what our language is really about) *given* his basic ontological categories.

This, I think, is the conclusion we must finally come to in our critique of Russell's program of analysis. But having pointed out its circularity we have not said everything that should be said concerning this program. For it is of utmost importance to realize that it is not simply an accident that this program is circular; in the last analysis *all* such programs must be circular.

There are, I would maintain, several possible ideal languages, not just one, each ideal *relative* to a particular set of ontological categories. Relative to one set of categories physical-object symbols may be basic; relative to another, symbols for sense-data; to another, symbols for universals – and so on. This, I think, puts the whole ideal language program in a new light. It indicates that the purpose of constructing an ideal language is not to exhibit the ontological structure of the world, but to show how the world appears *as delineated in terms of the basic categories of a particular philosophical system*. Thus the point of reconstructing language is not show what propositions "really" mean – in some absolute sense – but to show what they mean in terms of a particular categorical framework.

I conclude that our final evaluation of Russell's ideal language program will be determined, to a great extent, by our estimate of the soundness of his choice of basic ontological categories. This estimate, in turn, will depend in large part on our estimate of his fundamental epistemic commitments – to the theory of acquaintance and the certainty theory of knowing on which it is premised; for, as I have indicated, it was this commitment that led him to regard sense-data as a basic ontological category and hence to assume that the meaning of propositions of ordinary language must be rendered in terms of such entities. If our commitments coincide with those of Russell, the particular ideal language he envisages will likely seem to us an ultimate philosophical goal. If they do not, the quest for such a language, even as a theoretical goal, is likely to appear misguided, the result of some egregious philosophical confusion.

But taken as a whole, Russell's philosophy of language has, I think, great value, even for those philosophers who are unsympathetic to his basic commitments and categories. It is, in fact, something of a model for any philosopher who would attempt to pare off the misleading excresences of language to discover what, in terms of a particular set of categories, our propositions really mean. It shows us, that is, how to proceed in order to free ourselves from linguistically induced errors about the structure of reality.

SELECTED BIBLIOGRAPHY

Austin, J. L. "Truth," *Proceedings of the Aristotelian Society*, sup. v. XXIV (1950).

Ayer, A. J. (*et. al.*) *The Revolution in Philosophy*. London: Macmillan and Co., Ltd., 1956. Lectures by Ayer, W. C. Kneale, G. A. Paul, D. F. Pears, P. F. Strawson, G. J. Warnock, R. A. Wolheim.

Berlin, Isaiah. "Empirical Propositions and Hypothetical Statements," *Mind*, LIX (1950).

— "Logical Translation," *Proceedings of the Aristotelian Society*, L (1949–50).

Black, Max. "Russells' Philosophy of Language," In Schilpp (ed.) *The Philosophy of Bertrand Russell*.

Butchvarov, Panayot, "On an Alleged Mistake of Logical Atomism," *Analysis*, XIX (1959).

— "Meaning-as-Use and Meaning-as-Correspondence," *Philosophy*, XXXV (1960).

Carnap, Rudolf. *Meaning and Necessity*. Chicago: The University of Chicago Press, 1956.

— "Empiricism, Semantics, and Ontology," *Revue Internationale de Philisophie*, XI (1950). Reprinted in *Meaning and Necessity*.

Copilowish, Irving M. "Language Analysis and Metaphysical Inquiry," *Philosophy of Science*, XVI (1949).

Daitz, Edna. "The Picture Theory of Meaning," *Mind*, LXII (1953). Reprinted in Flew (ed.) *Essays in Conceptual Analysis*.

Feigl, H. and Sellars, W. (eds.) *Readings in Philosophical Analysis*. New York: Appleton-Century-Crofts, Inc., 1949.

Flew, A. G. N. (ed.) *Essays in Conceptual Analysis*. London: Macmillan and Co., Ltd., 1960.

— *Logic and Language*, I and II. Oxford; Basil Blackwell. First series, 1951; Second series, 1953.

Fritz, Charles A. *Bertrand Russell's Construction of the External World*. London: Routledge and Kegan Paul, 1952.

Geach, P. T. "Russell's Theory of Descriptions," in MacDonald (ed.) *Philosophy and Analysis*.

Gellner, Ernest. "Analysis and Ontology," *Philosophical Quarterly*, I (1950–51).

Hall, Everett. *Philosophical Systems*. Chicago: The University of Chicago Press, 1960.

Hampshire, Stuart. "Logical Form," *Proceedings of the Aristotelian Society*, XLVIII, (1947–48).

Hart, J. L. A. "Is There Knowledge by Acquaintance?" Symposium with J. N.

Findlay and G. E. Hughes. *Proceedings of the Aristotelian Society*, sup. v. XXIII (1949).

Herbst, Peter. "The Nature of Facts," in Flew (ed.) *Essays in Conceptual Analysis*.

Kalish, Donald. "Logical Form," *Mind*, LXI (1952).

Linsky, Leonard (ed.) *Semantics and the Philosophy of Language*. Urbana: The University of Illinois Press, 1952.

MacDonald, Margaret (ed.) *Philosophy and Analysis*. Oxford: University Press, 1954.

McClendon, J. C. "Uses of Similarity of Structure," *Mind* LXIV (1955).

Mill, John Stuart. *A System of Logic*. London: Longmans, Green and Co., 1936.

Moore, G. E. "Russell's Theory of Descriptions," in Schilpp (ed.) *The Philosophy of Bertrand Russell*.

Quine, W. V. O. "On What There Is," *Review of Metaphysics*, III (1948).

Quinton, Anthony. "Russell's Philosophical Development," *Philosophy*, XXXV (1960).

Reeves, J. W. "Origin and Consequences of the Theory of Descriptions," *Proceedings of the Aristotelian Society*, XXXIV (1933–34).

Russell, Bertrand. *A Critical Exposition of the Philosophy of Leibniz*. Cambridge: The University Press, 1900. Second edition, London: George Allen & Unwin, Ltd., 1937.

— *Introduction to Mathematical Philosophy*. London: George Allen & Unwin, Ltd., 1919.

— *Logic and Knowledge: Essays 1901–1950*. Edited by R. C. Marsh. London: George Allen & Unwin, Ltd., 1956.

— "Logical Atomism," in J. H. Muirhead (ed.) *Contemporary British Philosophy*. First Series, London: George Allen & Unwin, Ltd., 1924. Reprinted in *Logic and Knowledge*.

— "Mathematical Logic as Based on the Theory of Types," *American Journal of Mathematics*, XXX (1908). Reprinted in *Logic and Knowledge*.

— "Meinong's Theory of Complexes and Assumptions," *Mind*, XIII (1904).

— *My Philosophical Development*. London: George Allen & Unwin, Ltd., 1959.

— *Mysticism and Logic*. New York: Doubleday and Co., Inc., 1957. First edition, New York: 1918.

— "On Denoting," *Mind*, XIV (1905). Reprinted in *Logic and Knowledge*.

— "On Propositions: What They are and What They Mean," *Proceedings of the Aristotelian Society*, sup. v. II (1919). Reprinted in *Logic and Knowledge*.

— *Our Knowledge of the External World*. New York: The New American Library, 1960. First edition, London: 1914.

— "Philosophy of Logical Atomism," *Monist*, XXVIII (1918), XXIV (1919). Reprinted in *Logic and Knowledge*.

— *Principia Mathematica*. Volume I, with A. N. Whitehead. Cambridge: The University Press, 1910. Second edition: 1935.

— *Principles of Mathematics*. Cambridge: The University Press, 1903. Second edition, London: George Allen & Unwin, Ltd., 1938.

— *Problems of Philosophy*. New York: Oxford University Press, 1959. First edition, London: 1912.

Ryle, Gilbert. "Systematically Misleading Expressions," in Flew (ed.) *Logic and Language* (I).

— "The Theory of Meaning," in C. A. Mace (ed.) *British Philosophy in the Mid-Century*. London: George Allen & Unwin, Ltd., 1957.

Schilpp, P. A. (ed.) *The Philosophy of Bertrand Russell*. Evanston and Chicago: Northwestern University Press, 1944.

Sellars, Wilfrid. "Acquaintance and Description Again," *Journal of Philosophy*, XLVI (1949).

Shoemaker, Sydney. "Logical Atomism and Language," *Analysis* XX (1960).

Smullyan, Arthur. "Incomplete Symbols," *Philosophical Review*, LXVII (1958).

Stebbing, L. S. "Constructions," *Proceedings of the Aristotelian Society*, XXXIV (1933–34).

— "The Method of Analysis in Methaphysics," *Proceedings of the Aristotelian Society*, XXXIII (1932–33).

Strawson, P. F. *Introduction to Logical Theory*. London: Metheun and Co., Ltd., 1952.

— "On Referring," *Mind*, LIX (1950). Reprinted in Flew (ed.) *Essays in Conceptual Analysis*.

— "Review of *Logic and Knowledge*," *Philosophical Quarterly*, VII (1957).

Urmson, J. O. *Philosophical Analysis*. Oxford: The Clarendon Press, 1956.

Warnock, G. J. *English Philosophy Since 1900*. London: Oxford University Press, 1958.

— "Metaphysics in Logic," *Proceedings of the Aristotelian Society*, LI (1950–51). Reprinted in Flew (ed.) *Essays in Conceptual Analysis*.

Weitz, Morris. "Oxford Philosophy," *Philosophical Review*, LXII (1953).

— 'Review of Russell's *My Philosophical Development*," *Philosophical Review*, LXX (1961).

— "The Unity of Russell's Philosophy," in Schilpp (ed.) *The Philosophy of Bertrand Russell*.

Wisdom, John. "Logical Constructions, "*Mind*, XL (1931), XLI (1932), XLII (1933).

Wittgenstein, Ludwig. *Philosophical Investigations*. New York: The Macmillan Co., 1953.

— *Remarks of the Foundations of Mathematics*. Oxford: Basil Blackwell, 1956.

— *Tractatus Logico-Philosophicus*. London: Routledge and Kegan Paul, Ltd., 1922.